C000233300

LOVE BY NUMBERS

DR LUISA DILLNER is publishing director for new product development at the British Medical Journal Publishing Group. Published by the *Guardian*, *Observer*, *Sunday Telegraph*, *Cosmopolitan*, *Vogue* and *Elle*, she has also written for the famous Mumsnet website. She has four children, lives in London and most importantly has a perfect long term relationship.

LOVE BY NUMBERS

The hidden facts behind
everyone's relationships

DR LUISA DILLNER

PROFILE BOOKS

First published in Great Britain in 2009 by
PROFILE BOOKS LTD
3A Exmouth House
Pine Street
London ECIR OJH
www.profilebooks.com

This book is published in association with Guardian Books. Guardian
Books is an imprint of Guardian News & Media Limited. The Guardian is
a registered trademark of Guardian Media Group plc.

Copyright © Luisa Dillner, 2009

1 3 5 7 9 10 8 6 4 2

Printed in the UK by CPI Bookmarque, Croydon, CR0 4TD

The moral right of the author has been asserted.

All rights reserved. Without limiting the rights under copyright reserved
above, no part of this publication may be reproduced, stored or
introduced into a retrieval system, or transmitted, in any form or by any
means (electronic, mechanical, photocopying, recording or otherwise),
without the prior written permission of both the copyright owner and the
publisher of this book.

A CIP catalogue record for this book is available from the British Library.

ISBN 978 1 84668 073 1

Mixed Sources
Product group from well-managed
forests and other controlled sources
www.fsc.org Cert no. TT-COC-002227
© 1996 Forest Stewardship Council
FSC

For John, Sam, Madeleine, Mathilda, Lydia and my Mum;
all helped me to write this book

Contents

Introduction

This isn't a self-help book about relationships, so it won't tell you what to do. What it will do is answer, using facts and figures, many of the questions people have about relationships; and once you have this information, you can work most things out for yourself.

When I was a single parent with two children, I used to wonder if I'd ever meet someone new. It seemed unlikely, even without taking into account how useless I was (then) at relationships. Then one day I came across a newspaper report that said that 70 per cent of single parents were likely to find a new partner within five years. I was so surprised that I tore it out. It had never occurred to me that there'd be an answer to the question, 'Will I meet someone?' I'd thought it was down to chance, not that someone could make a well-informed prediction. Having prepared myself for years of maternal sacrifice I found myself thinking I was more likely to meet someone than not to. Maybe if the statistics said I would, I didn't even need to try. As it happens I met my partner at a friend's party (a good place, so the research tells us, but I have to thank my friend Janice who insisted I get out there) and have been with him ever since.

It was finding this statistic that made me wonder how much research there was about all the eternal, and unusual, questions about relationships: will I meet someone, should we move in together, should I have had that one-night stand, and so on. I'd been working as a doctor, firstly in hospitals and then for the *British Medical Journal*, and everyone was talking about 'evidence-based medicine'. There was a big push for doctors to make sure they were treating people on the basis of the best research evidence. If this was such a good thing, why, I wondered, didn't we use it to inform other areas of our lives? When I heard people telling their friends what to do about their boyfriends, husbands, wives or girlfriends, I couldn't help thinking, 'But how do you know?'

We may think that our feelings about relationships, and especially love, are unique – that no one goes through what we're going through. How we feel about Tom, Dick or Harriet is sometimes (especially to our friends) inexplicable. But even so we'll often sound out our friends, who are usually game enough to offer an opinion, based mostly on their sometimes limited experience. What we may not realize is that there are lots of research studies that show what happened not just to a couple of people but sometimes hundreds, who have had similar relationship dilemmas to the ones we're having. Research in these areas occasionally makes it into the broadsheet pages of the national press, but the vast majority of similar findings are not known to the public.

When I started writing the *Guardian* column 'Love by Numbers', on which this book is based, instead of just giving an opinion like traditional agony aunt columns, I wanted to see if I could provide quantitative answers. And looking for research about relationships, I was surprised how much there was – and how quirky some of it was. There is research on whether men will leave their partners for their mistresses (they usually won't), whether open marriages make people happier (they don't), and how often attempts to 'poach someone' are successful (around 50 per cent of the time). Researchers, mostly social psychologists, have hidden in park bushes to see whether couples without children are more affectionate to each other than lovers encumbered by kids (they are). They have scanned college yearbooks to see whether women who smile in their photo are happier in their relationships than those who don't (they are). And then there are the relationship experts like John M. Gottman, who watches couples in his love lab, identifying precisely the ones most likely to split up by listening for just a few minutes to how they talk to each other and applying a mathematical formula.

Some of the conclusions seemed obvious, but most of it was surprising. Perhaps the most surprising thing is that the research, from academic journals (such as the *Journal of Personality and Social Psychology*, the *Journal of Marriage and Family* and *Sex Roles*), think tanks, government reports and statistical offices, answers the everyday questions we all have about relationships. Does having children ruin them? What's the best way of finding someone? Do opposites attract? Is there such a thing as a soul mate?

Not all research is created equal: papers vary in quality, and some samples are more representative than others (psychologists have a habit of using their students for research, and they are not always like the rest of us). The research in this book is international, but a lot of it comes from America and Britain because many of the research centres and journals are based in these countries. I've tried to include the most useful evidence and to describe any shortcomings it might have. Sometimes the evidence comes from surveys, and it's hard to know who will have taken part. Even the best studies have their limitations, and their findings can only give you more information – not a definitive answer. But often knowing what has happened to other people can shed some light on what might happen to you and what you can do about it.

Many of the letters I get sent for the *Guardian* column are about sex, often from men saying they're not getting enough (which makes you wonder if any men ever do). One letter was from a woman saying that now she'd had a baby, her husband wanted more sex to make up for the time they'd lost. 'I just want to sleep,' she wrote. 'I don't like to ask what the mothers in playgroup are doing.' It's a shame she didn't know, because they're almost certainly doing the same as she is – having less sex than they used to. If men don't ever get enough sex, women don't ever get enough help with childcare and the housework. And guess what – the two, as we'll see, are related.

People often ask if having a second go with someone is likely to work, or if someone who's left them will come back. I think back to how I used to tell friends that their ex might change their mind; now I'd tell them it's pretty unlikely. That's because the research shows that someone who physically leaves a relationship has usually emotionally left a few months earlier. Some of the letters are sad – why do people have affairs with their partner's best friends? – but most of them are enquiring and optimistic.

I don't get many letters from gay people, which is a shame as there's a growing research base in this area. Some of the research is applicable to gay relationships but some research shows that these relationships are different – they tend to be more equal and, for example, use more humour in arguments – but as more research is done on different types of relationships, we'll learn more about the similarities and differences. The people who write, gay or straight, increasingly ask for facts and figures – I'd be surprised if agony aunts in general get asked for the evidence for their answers.

Sifting through the research has made me think I haven't been terribly good at relationships. There are various habits that are particularly destructive to couples, and I've been guilty of a few of them. I now no longer shriek, 'You never do anything around the house!' and instead go for a more gentle, 'It would really help me if you could do the hoovering.' I avoid resurrecting rows from five years ago when arguing about something unrelated, and have reluctantly given up nasty name calling. I try to remember my partner is a person too, who has his own hopes and fears, however inconvenient these may be. Sadly, I realize, relationships are not all about me, after all.

One thing my partner and I have always been good at is having a laugh during an argument, which the research rather pleasingly says is a good thing. Sometimes he'll say, 'You're only doing this because you've read some research that says you should.' Well, I reply, that's a good thing, isn't it? Once you've read this book, you may want to hide it, to avoid similar accusations.

Mr or Mrs Right

CHAT-UP LINES

I've never been any good at chatting up women. A friend suggested some chat-up lines that work for him but sound gross to me. He's very good-looking so women probably don't care what he's saying. But can chat-up lines work and, if so, which ones are they?

There is a science to chat-up lines. A chat-up line works if it shows you off to some advantage, by making you look interesting, humorous, athletic or rich. Preferably all of the above. The risk is that the wrong line, even if delivered from a Brad Pitt lookalike, will be met with ridicule. The type of ridicule that can haunt you for ever. But on the bright side, there are tips to be had, because there's been research on the best chat-up lines. Questions seem to work better than statements. A study of 100 people (aged from twenty-two to forty-five years of age) who went on three-minute speed dates were asked to pick the best opening lines they heard. The researchers, from the University of Hertfordshire, were generous enough to share the results. The winning chat-up lines? 'What is your favourite pizza topping?' and 'Who would you be if you were going on *Stars in Your Eyes?*' These lines give the other person the chance to respond in a light-hearted way. Something that the worst chat-up lines ('I have a PhD in computing' and 'My best friend is a helicopter pilot') failed to do.

More-detailed research into chat-up lines has been undertaken based on hypothetical stories. A study of 205 undergraduates by psychologists at the University of Edinburgh asked them to rank chat-up lines from made-up scenarios. Women liked the one where a man at a trendy bar says, 'I'm one of the owners here, would you like to dance?' thus showing off wealth and dancing ability, two highly desirable qualities in one sentence. The use of these scenarios may bias the study, however. In one of them, in which a man protects a woman from two lager louts, you'd have to think any chat-up line would be a winner; even 'I have a PhD in computing.'

Men, bless them, like to use sexual chat-up lines, as in 'If I said you had a beautiful body would you hold it against me?' and 'I may not be Fred Flintstone but I bet I could make your Bed Rock,' or the even less poetic 'Is there a mirror in your knickers? I think I can see myself in them.' This, the research tells us, is their subtle way of finding a woman who wants a shag. Women say they prefer chat-up lines that show a man could have more long-term potential. Therefore any opening line that shows off wealth (which studies show is something women still find strangely appealing in a partner), a generous nature, and confidence (in a realistic way, so not 'Shall I buy an island?') is attractive. Empty compliments don't seem to work, although lines such as 'Do you know the number for the Ordnance Survey? I've just found a site of outstanding beauty,' have a cheesy charm.

Whatever chat-up line you use, make sure that you smile when you say it. Smiling increases your chances of a positive response and some people will have made up their mind about you before you've opened your mouth.

ONLINE MATING

Is internet dating a good way of meeting someone? I haven't had a relationship with anyone since I split up from my boyfriend three years ago. I don't want to be on my own and online dating seems more acceptable than it used to be. How successful is it likely to be? I'm thirty-five years old.

The internet is one of the most common ways for people to find dates. A survey by Nielsen/NetRatings on meeting people put it third after 'through friends' and 'in pubs and clubs' and estimated that three and a half million people a month use dating websites. Around 11 per cent of us who use the internet visit a dating site each month. And why not? You can do it from home (initially), 24 hours a day (if you have the stamina), it's relatively safe and anonymous (if you're careful) and no longer just for those who are desperate. It's now cool to find your true love online. And although some people sign up to find 'friends' and have flings, a survey by topdates. com found that 6 per cent of their users have married their online partners. A Pew Internet Study in the US of over 3,000 adults found that 15 per cent knew someone in a long-term relationship that had started online. Match.com say that 200,000 people a month find someone on their site.

A more academically robust study of 229 online daters by Dr Jeff Gavin from Bath University showed that their most significant online relationship lasted on average for seven months, with a quarter lasting a year. Dr Gavin says that success rates are similar to offline methods but that the opportunity for people to remain anonymous for a while is an advantage. People feel they can express their emotions more readily online, which can accelerate intimacy. However, people can also lie more easily. They tend to do this in real life as well as online but extending the truth is easier online because it's less real. Studies show that people most commonly lie about weight, age and, oh yes, being married. Some lie more spectacularly, Karen Carlton, a divorcee in Fife, lived for two years with a former US Marine she met online, before she found out he was a fantasist from Leicester.

If you have reasonable expectations, online dating is a good way to start looking for dates. Sensible precautions apply as they do in offline life: don't give away too much about yourself, meet in a public place (lunch is good, as you can get away earlier if required), choose profiles with photos. Beware of men who only 'wink' at you on sites (time wasters), call themselves 'Top Gun' or email 'My life was meaningless without you; I think of you every minute of every day,' within the first week, since this is not normal. Increase your success rate by posting a photo and a truthful profile. Online dating agencies advise looking friendly rather than seductive or cross in photos, as approachability increases success rates. Best of all, use a dictionary when composing your profile. One of the biggest turn-offs, apparently, is profiles with poor spelling.

SPEEDY DATING

I'm twenty-six years old and split up from my girlfriend eight months ago. Since then I've been single. I've considered speed dating but I'm worried that no one will choose to see me again. Is there anything I can do to increase my chances of success?

One of the joys of speed dating is that it's safe from instant rejection. No woman will dismiss you to your face. You usually only hear if you've had any matches (if someone you want to see also wants to see you again) a couple of days after the event. And you should get at least one match at an event. Ever since Rabbi Yaacov Deyo invented speed dating in Los Angeles in 1998 to help Jewish singles get together it has been frequently studied. Most speed daters haven't met each other before – so these are random meetings, albeit among people who select themselves by choosing to go speed dating – and by finding out how speed daters then choose each other researchers can work out what attracts people to each other. At least at a speed dating event. As you'll see, it's not so different from real life – just even more superficial.

So prepare to be underwhelmed. To be successful you'll need to be tall, young, slim and good-looking. A recent study from Essex University of 3,600 men and women attending speed dating events found that every 2.5 cm of height a man had over other men increased his chances of being picked by 5 per cent. In studies of what people look for in long-term partners, they'll say 'kindness, intelligence and an attractive personality'. Well, speed daters leave some of that touchy-feely nonsense at home. The 3- or 4-minute time limit on each date means that market forces apply. Education and income have little influence, although other studies show that thin, tall people are more likely to have higher incomes. About two thirds of speed daters in the studies have degrees; the national average is 20 per cent. A study in *Evolution and Human Behavior* of over 10,500 people who took part in HurryDate sessions in America also found that both sexes cared most about physical appearance and that few people were picked on the basis of their income, personality or wealth.

Be warned that women are choosier than men; they chose two to three men per session and saw 45 per cent of their choices matched. Men chose five women and had 20 per cent matched. A third of men but only 11 per cent of women got no matches. Many people don't choose anyone; those who think they are less desirable may pick more people as matches to increase their chances of getting a date with someone.

How successful speed dating is at generating long-term relationships is less clear because these studies have yet to be done, but a study from Northwestern University in America published in *Personal Relationships* found that 163 undergraduate speed daters embarked on over 500 dates afterwards. Not exactly long-term follow-up, but it shows enthusiasm.

As in all markets your success depends on the competition, but wear shoe raises, hold in your stomach, look young, and have a nice, friendly face and you'll get lots of interest. Your personality will only matter on any of the dates that hopefully follow.

ROMANTIC TIMING

I'm a single forty-something male who recently joined a dating website. After an indifferent start I was told by a female friend that women are not interested in beginning new relationships in the winter and that spring is the best time for this. Is this true? Are relationships more likely to begin at different times of the year? Should I wait until the clocks change?

Spring always feels like such a hopeful season, doesn't it? So full of promise. Yet strangely it doesn't feature as a peak time of activity for dating websites. The most popular times for people to sign up for dating agencies are January, February (in the aftermath of a barren Valentine's day) and the second week of September, says Mary Balfour, managing director of the dating agency Drawing Down the Moon. Balfour also works on the online agency loveandfriends.com (135,000 members) and believes that the peaks reflect people's needs to reassess their relationship status shortly after Christmas (no one to kiss under the mistletoe) and at the end of summer (after ill-judged holiday romances). Match.com (20 million members worldwide) says their busiest day ever was 6 January last year, reflecting a rush of New Year's resolutions to find a mate.

Balfour's view of spring being the best month to launch an online romantic assault is 'It's a load of rubbish.' If you've had an indifferent start to online dating you should blame your profile or photograph rather than the season. Photographs are essential – you are twelve times more likely to get approached if someone can see what you look like. Try to look friendly rather than moodily handsome, and while we're at it your profile should be flirty (not sleazy) and humorous. If you update your profile it moves you up the search-engine hierarchy, so more people will find you. There's apparently a shortage of single men in their forties, so rather than wait for lambs to gambol in the fields and daffodils to bloom, just make sure you come across as half decent and normal.

That you shouldn't wait for spring is further (if weakly) backed up by a survey of over 1,000 people by Scripps Howard News Service in America. It found that over half of the people in their survey thought spring no more romantic than any other season although men were slightly more dewy-eyed about it. There's an argument that December, with its lack of daylight and the magic of Christmas, is the most romantic month, which is borne out by the fact that it usually has the highest rates of conception, although there are also less romantic explanations for this involving alcohol and unprotected sex.

There's a feeling among social anthropologists that autumn should be the peak time for trying to find a mate, because as life goes back to normal once the summer holidays are over and the nights draw in you want a steady relationship. Someone to cook with and snuggle up with under the duvet. Someone to nest with.

But we don't know when the peak season is for actual success in romance – we only know about activity. So if you want a relationship you shouldn't wait for some optimum time that doesn't exist. The reality is that clocks have little to do with it. Be it Greenwich Mean Time or not, what matters is that the timing's right for both of you.

IN THE STARS?

I'm a 28-year-old man who is having a great relationship with a lovely woman for the first time in five years. The only problem is that she's into horoscopes – she reads them every day. She's delighted that our signs are compatible but I wonder if she would be so keen if they weren't. There is no evidence that your sign determines who you are attracted to, is there?

The short answer is no, don't be stupid; but there's a longer one. This is because horoscopes are sufficiently irritating to provoke researchers into providing evidence to disprove them. Which is just as well because many people believe them. A 2004 survey reported in the *Guardian* newspaper of 3,000 young people aged between eighteen and twenty-four showed that two thirds believed in horoscopes, compared with a third who believed in the Bible. A survey of 1,122 art students and 383 science students at York University in Toronto found that 92 per cent knew their star sign (What planet had the others been on? My seven-year-old daughter knows she's a Leo), and a quarter of arts and 1 in 5 science students had made a conscious decision based on their horoscope in the past year. Since horoscopes are vague, as in 'Be careful what you wish for, being wealthy does not necessarily bring happiness', one wonders what decisions they made. A study by the French statistician Michel Gauquelin sent the characteristics for the horoscope for one of the worst mass murderers in French history to 150 people and asked how well it fitted them – 94 per cent said they recognized themselves in the description.

It is clearly annoying to think you have been chosen for your star sign, but since 500 million people share that sign, you can still take some personal credit. If someone truly believes that as a Pisces they are best off with a Scorpio then they may look out for or at least be receptive to people with that star sign. But any activity along these lines is marginal. A study by Dr David Voas at the University of Manchester analysed the birthdays of 20 million husbands and wives using data from the 2001 Census. It found no evidence that astrological signs had any impact on the probability of marrying someone of any other sign. If there had been even a small influence, such as 1 in 1,000 influenced by the stars, then he calculated we would see 10,000 more couples than expected with certain combinations of star signs. But there weren't. Astrologers criticized his study for not looking at full birth charts (with birth dates and times) but, as Voas says, he used the same criteria as are used in astrologers' columns. Perhaps most interesting was that Voas found a random distribution of birthday combinations – so that even a belief in astrology didn't influence people in their marriage choices. If your only problem with your girlfriend is that she believes in horoscopes then things are going pretty well and you can rest easy in the knowledge that whatever she thinks, your star sign is not what makes you compatible. The only thing I'd be worried about is what else your girlfriend believes in. Check out where she stands on dragons and flying saucers.

BIRTH ORDER

I am the oldest child and my boyfriend is the youngest in his family. I have heard that the order in which you are born into your family influences your personality, who you should choose as a partner and even if you become gay. Is there anything in this?

There's something in birth order but the question is how much. Parents treat their oldest and youngest children differently – the latter getting more relaxed upbringings. Dr Kevin Leman, a psychologist with a research interest in birth order, says that first-borns are natural leaders, who take responsibility, are more likely to have fewer sexual partners and fully commit to making relationships work. (It's an often quoted statistic that most US presidents are first-borns.) They are, it is said, the ones most likely to marry their childhood sweethearts. This conformity, however, makes them less spontaneous (for that read dull in bed) but committed to going the distance. Now, the good news for you is that their best match is with a youngest child. This is because a youngest child is fun (they got to go out all night because their parents were too worn out to argue) and loving (the youngest gets the cuddles), but they appreciate the parental qualities that first-borns often possess. Younger children can have issues of laziness – the youngest child gets everything done for them. But then oldest children have a controlling issue (so stalemate when two first-borns get together). Middle children work hard at relationships (because they were never treated as special – so they tend to compromise and work hard) and twins make

understanding partners because they've always had someone
else to think about. Children without brothers and sisters are
super dependable and supportive.

However much we might recognize some of these personality
traits, we're as likely to think of as many exceptions to as
examples of the rules, and the research doesn't back up some
of the traits. A study from Florida Atlantic University of 438
men and women in the journal *Personality and Individual
Differences* found that first-borns had more sexual partners
than later born children. In support of the commitment
theory of first-borns, they wanted children at a younger age
than those lower down the birth order. But there were no
differences in when first and later born children settled down
in long-term relationships.

There is considerable research looking at birth order and
sexual preference. A study of over 87,000 men and 71,000
women by the University of Toronto, done through a BBC
internet survey, found that having older brothers increased
the likelihood of a man being homosexual but specifically
for men who were not right-handed (so either left-handed or
ambidextrous). Each older brother, the study found, increased
the likelihood of being homosexual by 15 per cent. Birth order
had no effect on women's sexuality.

However strong or weak the effect of birth order on
relationships, there isn't much you can do about it. Nothing,
actually. And using 'Where do you come in your family?' as a
chat-up line is as bad as asking someone about their star sign.

WANTED: HANDSOME MEN

I have been looking for a relationship for some time but I don't meet many men who I find that good-looking, and looks are important to me. I see many more good-looking women than men. This isn't because I think the women I know are attractive just because I know their personalities. I do care about men's personalities, but do men have more choice when it comes to good-looking partners?

At the risk of sexual stereotyping, women may still make more of an effort when they go out and hence seem better looking. However, evolutionary psychologists (who research how evolution might have made us how we are) think there's some evidence that there really are more beautiful women than gorgeous looking men in the world. This fits with the Trivers-Willard hypothesis, beloved of evolutionary psychologists, that says parents who have any inheritable trait that is good for a particular sex will have more children of that sex. Robert Trivers, an American evolutionary biologist, and Dan Willard, a mathematician, reckoned that tall, strong fathers would have more sons because hunter-gatherers did better against wild bison if they were bigger. Sons can also have more children (they don't have to do the pregnancy bit) and spread these desirable genes. Women who are young, not too tall, with symmetrical facial features and normal body weight (women forever get it wrong about men wanting size zero girlfriends) are more likely to have girls because these factors are associated with fertility. And fertility is a woman's greatest asset, evolutionarily speaking. In short, men look for above average in looks and average in other areas for long-term partners. Women (and I am just repeating the body of evidence) go for looks more in the short-term and money (as well as good communication skills and a sense of humour) long-term.

In a study of 3,000 Americans from the Longitudinal Study of Adolescent Health by Satoshi Kanazawa from the London School of Economics, the attractiveness of parents was rated on a five-point scale (there is evidence that there is a lot of global agreement on what constitutes good looks). He found that parents rated 'very attractive' were 26 per cent less likely to have a son, having taken other factors such as education and number of sexual partners into account. What this means of course is that if better looking people have more daughters than sons, women will continue to get better looking while men, well, won't. But men may think they are good-looking anyway. In this study 28 per cent of this sample rated themselves as 'very attractive' whereas only 11 per cent were so rated by the researcher.

This study has been criticized on statistical grounds for being more speculative than scientifically proven, and there are many people who are sniffy about evolutionary psychology. But feel free to take this as some evidence that you're right. However, looks are only part of what's attractive about someone. There are many other psychology studies that support the more developed view that if you like someone's personality you'll rate them as better looking. So you could try that too and see if it works.

REELING FROM REJECTION

I'm 26-years-old and ready to embark on a serious, fulfilling relationship with a man. I am a very passionate person and cannot hold back when I really feel for someone. I've recently met a man who had bowled me over to the extent that if it were to fail in the near future I don't think I would recover for what would possibly be a few months. This has caused me to consider whether I am not the kind of person who is able to have relationships at all.

It's normal to be a bit scared of getting hurt by a relationship, but not to be so terrified that you'd rather not risk one at all. Getting dumped is an almost universal experience and most people bounce back (a few months isn't so long), believing that it'll work out with someone else. If you are over-sensitive to rejection you will take being dumped too personally. If he dumps you, you may assume that anyone you get involved with will too. And hey, let's not stop there – maybe no one likes you. You'll end up working from the premise that to know you is not to like you which ends up being a self-fulfilling prophecy. Instead you need to believe, as most people do, that next time it will be different.

Psychologists say that our ability to deal with rejection is based on how we learn to attach ourselves to people, mostly as children. If you have a fearful attachment style then you will be overly anxious that closeness leads to rejection. This is not good for your mental health. A study by Professor Toni Bifulco at the University of London asked 222 women who had been identified as having a higher risk of depression by their family doctor to fill out a questionnaire on attachment style based on a global scale. Bifulco found that those with fearful attachment styles were nearly three times more likely to become depressed within twelve months than those with 'secure' attachment styles. So you need to find ways to stop feeling like this, as it's destructive.

Other studies show that if you are sensitive to rejection you will trash your relationships, seeing rejection where it doesn't exist and driving your partner bonkers by over-reacting to perceived slights. People who are preoccupied with being rejected tend to be unhappier in relationships because they expect them to end and are anxious, jealous and controlling – all recognized ways of tipping relationships into oblivion. You can get professional help – cognitive behavioural therapy may help you think more positively about yourself and your relationships, for example – but you can start with friends you can trust, checking your view of reality out against their view. Then you can re-set your sensitivity gauge. Since you don't know this man very well yet, why not re-set your passion gauge as well. You can't really be mad about someone before you get to know them. So in the interests of self-preservation, tread more cautiously.

NICE GUY BUT …

I'm not successful with women, although I've got many female friends. The women I want to go out with seem to prefer men who treat them badly. My friends say I'm too nice. Don't women want to date nice guys?

What is a nice guy? In various studies women define nice men as anything from kind, considerate and loyal to passive, sexually inexperienced and boring. Women also use 'too nice', euphemistically, to reject men they really think are too dull. Women do want to date nice guys, when nice means something positive and not just wet, but the studies showing this are not that helpful. They are based on surveys of men with characteristics that women say they would date rather than who they actually do date. And hypothetical scenarios don't always come that close to real-life reactions.

For example, a study in the journal *Sex Roles* put three scenarios to forty-eight female undergraduates at an American liberal arts college. Their average age was twenty (another limitation). The women had scripted answers from hypothetical men to the question, 'What is your definition of a real man?' The 'nicest' man said he was in touch with his and his partner's feelings, was kind and put his partner's pleasure in the bedroom first. The middle nice one said he was good to the woman he loved. And the third said he didn't go in for touchy feely stuff. So guess who won? Mr Nicest man was chosen not only as the best boyfriend but as top husband and platonic friend. When the study used photos of men of varying attractiveness alongside these answers, being good-looking and the nicest man sent his scores through the roof.

But nice men may do less well in the real world because they don't pursue women, won't talk them into a date and never grab. Many people exaggerate the truth to within a whisker of a lie to get themselves a date; a nice guy reduces his chances because he wouldn't dream of cheating in that way. The adage of treating someone mean to keep (or even get) them keen is not an option for a nice guy – so don't even think about it because you'll be rubbish at it anyway.

Nice on its own is not enough; women want good-looking, interesting, fun and passionate. The amount of nice-ness that's desirable depends on the vacant position – it's vital for a long-term partner but not essential for a casual fling. Studies show that women prefer risk-taking and unreliable men for short-term relationships. But nice is a great attribute and you'll get a date eventually. Work on some of the other things that women want, such as being interesting, confident and making the most of your appearance, and you'll get one even faster.

BLONDE OR BRUNETTE?

My friend is blonde, and although we are both quite attractive she gets more attention from men when we go out together. Is it true that gentlemen prefer blondes?

The evidence for whether men prefer blondes is not that robust, coming as it does from evolutionary psychology, which is often sneered at by scientists, and research by, for example, City University, which while sound, is funded by Sunsilk, purveyors of fine hair products. You could try watching the classic musical *Gentlemen Prefer Blondes* (originally a novel) starring Jane Russell as the brunette and Marilyn Monroe as the blonde and come to your own conclusions. And think of Barbie – is she a brunette? I don't think so.

We can start with some other research from the City
University study in which 468 men were asked to describe
the same model, who was wearing digitally enhanced blonde,
brown and red hair. Blonde women were described as less
intelligent but more approachable. A total of 53 per cent
thought most people found blondes more attractive, but they
said they themselves had no preference. Out of those who did
have a preference, they preferred women to have the same
colour hair as they did – so blonde men preferred fair-haired
women. There may be bias in this study as men may have
thought they'd look shallow picking the blonde. But would
that worry them? A study from the University of Coventry
asked 120 people to rate a model for characteristics such
as intelligence and popularity. The model scored lowest for
intelligence when wearing a platinum blonde wig, but she won
the popularity vote.

Studies show cultural differences in ideal body shape, but
I couldn't find any research specifically looking at hair
colour in countries other than western ones. A study in the
Scandinavian *Journal of Psychology* of 130 men and 112 women
asked them to rate twelve drawings of people with varying
skin and hair colour. Brunettes and fairer skinned-people were
rated most highly.

There is an argument though that Ice Age man preferred
blondes. An evolutionary paper by the Canadian
anthropologist Peter Frost in the journal *Evolution and Human
Behavior* argues that in northern Europe 11,000 years ago
there was a male shortage due to deaths while out hunting.
In the scrum for mates blonde women stood out because
there were less of them and their hair shone in the sunlight
and so they were picked more by men. Frost also cites studies
showing that blonde hair darkens more slowly with age and
is thus associated with youth and fertility, another reason for

the attraction of blondes. So northern Europe developed a diversity of hair (and also eye) colour over a relatively short time (conditions were different in other continents). Frost argues this over twelve pages citing the MC1R gene colour (which you can't get out of a bottle) as being responsible for the variation in Europe's hair colour.

So blondes may have had the edge but the tide's now turned. Worse, there have been media reports quoting the World Health Organization as saying natural blondes are dying out (due to the MC1R gene being a feeble, recessive gene and because men find blondes out of a bottle more attractive than the genuine article). The last blonde was predicted to be born in Finland in 2202. But if you are a bitter brunette (and I'm not saying you are) don't take any comfort from this. It was all a hoax. The WHO even issued what must be its strangest press release. 'WHO.....would like to stress that we have no opinion on the future existence of blondes.'

DIM VIEW

I find guys who wear glasses a bit of a turn-off. I have good eyesight and I'd like my children to inherit this. My heart sinks when I realize a date is wearing contact lenses. I realize I'm cutting down my chances of meeting a soul mate by rejecting the increasing number of men in their thirties wearing glasses. What are the odds my offspring will have good eyesight if my future partner doesn't?

It isn't possible to give exact odds because geneticists think both short- and long-sightedness are caused by a combination of dodgy genes and environmental factors. A study at St Thomas' Hospital in London that looked at the DNA of 221 pairs of identical and non-identical twins found people with myopia (short-sightedness) had faults in the PAX6 gene which controls how the eye develops. Previous research estimates that inherited factors account for 89 per cent of the risk for short-sightedness and the environment accounts for 11 per cent. But that won't give your children their personal odds. When my mother said, 'Don't sit so close to the TV, it will ruin your eyes,' I didn't believe her and thought she was just trying to ruin my life. But it turns out that a child's risk of short-sightedness is increased by sitting too close to the TV, playing on game consoles and even reading too much (although there is no definition of too much). In the UK 1 in 4 people are short-sighted, according to data from the World Health Organization. Don't fall for a Singaporean, as up to 80 per cent of young men in Singapore are short-sighted.

But having kids who need specs is the least of your worries, because there are worse things that can happen to someone than needing minor visual assistance. If in your survey for a partner you've got tick boxes that just say 'soul mate', 'good-looking', 'great in bed', 'makes me laugh', then your ambition is clearly limited. Why not include 'no family history of heart disease, depression, alcoholism or diabetes'? All these carry an increased risk for your child's long-term health. While you're at it, ask your next boyfriend to draw a family tree to make sure no one's died early from any rare genetic disorders. Families sometimes forget that stuff. And why stop there? Whatever happened to screening boyfriends for their earning potential and likelihood of inheriting money? You wouldn't want your children suffering from any diseases caused by poverty.

We are all biologically driven to get the best genes for our kids. Anthropologists cite shiny haired, slim women as being desirable because they scream, 'I've got good genes and can give you perfect healthy babies.' You will know that there are no guarantees that any baby you have will be healthy, or that they will grow up untouched by any illness or hardship. Perhaps your wish to screen as much as possible beforehand reflects some deeper anxieties about motherhood. If you don't find men with glasses or contact lenses attractive then so be it. But if you do reject a guy that you like because he is visually challenged, then it's you who are the short-sighted one.

BIG EGOS

I am attracted to conventionally good-looking men who have large egos, and I worry I will never meet someone with whom I can be in a committed relationship. The men I show an interest in run a mile when they realize I would like something long-term with them. Can men with large egos ever feel love for someone other than themselves?

Most women are attracted to good-looking men – so no mystery there. It's the supersize ego that's the problem. While a strong sense of self is fine, someone bordering on the narcissistic is not well suited to committed relationships. The research shows that people who love themselves too much usually hope there will be someone even better for their image in the next bar, however charming and absorbed in you they seem at the outset. The men you describe (and there are women too) won't modify their behaviour in relationships because they can't see what's in it for them. They certainly don't want intimacy. Yuck.

Researchers from the University of Georgia carried out a study to see if narcissistic people ever thought their partners were less committed than they themselves were in their relationship. They asked 154 female students who were in relationships to list reasons why their partners might be either more or less committed to them. Those who scored higher on scales of narcissism found it twice as hard to think of reasons why their partner would be unhappy as opposed to reasons for their being happy with them. They felt pretty good about their relationship, however bad their partner felt. But this was largely because they couldn't imagine how anyone could be less than delighted by them.

Can people like this change? Perhaps only in Hollywood films where they get shot or have a brain haemorrhage and as they fight for life realize they're self-centred jerks and change into committed partners. But I wouldn't rely on this.

You're not a doormat for liking men with large egos; these men are popular. They are attractive for their enormous self-belief and outgoing personalities. But they don't want a real relationship, more a brief fling. Such people may not even realize the pain they cause, being so wrapped up in themselves. But while it's not your fault that you find these men attractive you can still apply the brakes. Make sure you let relationships develop in their own time, through the initial attraction and 'that's absolutely fascinating' to the reality of being a couple. Commitment isn't something that anyone who is normal signs up to after the first few dates. Researchers from the University of Denver developed a scale to measure it, breaking commitment down into dedication (I want to make our relationship work for both of us), constraint (why look for anyone else when I have you?) and satisfaction. It found that couples could be extremely committed but not that satisfied with their relationships. So even if you have commitment you still have to work on being happy together.

You are likely to meet someone right for a long-term relationship, and you'll know when it happens because he will act committed. So be more selective. Go for a normal man – the vast majority really can love someone other than themselves.

FREUDIAN BLIP

I have read on more than one occasion that men are likely to choose partners who remind them of their mothers. What if I in no way resemble his mother? Will the relationship last?

Are you sure you don't resemble your partner's mother? It's oedipal to think of him wanting to go out with his mother but sweet to think he might want someone a bit like her. Researchers claim that both men and women are susceptible to sexual imprinting, defined as the sexual preference we have for individuals who look like our (opposite-sex) parent. The hypothesis is that by looking into someone's face as an infant you get a template by which to judge your future mate. But it's sex specific. Men don't want a lover who looks like their dad.

The adage that men should look at their wives' mothers to see how their partner will age is apparently out of date. Men should look at their own mums. This is shown by research in 2002 by Tamás Bereczkei, a Hungarian psychologist who compared over 300 pictures of faces of family members with those of strangers. The people who acted as the judges in the study correctly matched wives to their husband's mothers more often than by chance (significantly so).

In a more recent study by Bereczkei, in the Proceedings of the Royal Society B., he identified more specifically the facial characteristics that people most look for in partners (when they're unconsciously looking for a mummy or daddy substitute). His team measured the facial proportions of 312 people from fifty-two Hungarian families. The matches between family members (which included a young man or woman, their long-term partner and both sets of parents) were compared with those of randomly selected couples by independent judges. (It sounds more complicated than it is.) They found that young women resembled their partner's mothers in terms of how full their lips were, the width of their mouths and the size of their jaws. Women went for men who had their dad's nose and a similar jaw-length to face-length ratio. This has to be unconscious, unless your partner's taken a tape measure to the lower part of your face.

But the desire men seem to have for their mothers is not merely skin deep. Men want to have long-term relationships with women who are as smart as their mothers. A study by sociologist Christine Whelan at the University of Iowa surveyed 800 men who earned salaries in the top 10 per cent of their age group (they were in their twenties and thirties) and found that nearly 80 per cent of those whose mothers had bachelor degrees had wives who were educated to a similar level.

However, even if you can't find anything in common with your partner's mother there's no need to worry. There are many reasons why relationships last: how well you deal with conflict, how you share the housework, whether you have a laugh together, and what your sex life is like. I've yet to see a list that includes how much you resemble his mother.

Opportunity Knocks

POACHED PARTNERS

I met this woman who's a friend of a friend and I really like her. She's been seeing a guy and is about to move in with him. I'm twenty-eight, single and everyone I meet these days is taken. Is it wrong to go after her? She can always say no.

Is it wrong? It's certainly rude – like sneezing into someone else's soup. Trying to pinch someone else's partner is called 'mate poaching' by relationship researchers, and for an underhand, emotionally fraught and morally dodgy activity it is remarkably popular.

There's a lot of data on this. David Schmitt from Bradley University in America led a study covering fifty-three countries that asked nearly 17,000 people if they'd ever tried to poach someone's partner or if someone had tried to poach them. On average the study, in the *Personality and Social Psychology Bulletin*, shows that 60 per cent of men and 40 per cent of women have tried to poach someone. In Asian and

Middle Eastern countries the rates were lower than in the West. Nearly two thirds of people said that someone had tried to poach them. If you want to know your chances of success with poaching, around 50 per cent of people who had a poaching attempt made on them went along with it. Men were more likely to do so than women, especially if it looked like a short-term poach – it's like having someone on loan.

There's no reason why poaching shouldn't result in a longer relationship; although usually it doesn't. In previous studies of American college students (but replicated in older populations), Schmitt has shown that 15 per cent of all current relationships started off as mate poaching.

There is an evolutionary element to this, which isn't an excuse because we all know better now, but in times of war, famine and pestilence lots of people lost their partners while they were relatively young. Most of the attractive people left were taken so people had to poach. In traditional hunter-gathering cultures, according to Schmitt, mate poaching is common.

The methods that poachers use are simple but effective. One study refers to the poacher 'slowly invading the target's social network'. This means sidling up to her friends. Other methods include sowing seeds of dissatisfaction, such as sighing sympathetically and insincerely and saying, 'I'm not sure your partner really appreciates you.' Overt flirting is a no-no, as would-be poachers risk getting a bloody nose from a jealous partner. During this underhand activity you'll have to make sure your friends don't rumble you. No one likes a poacher because no one wants someone to swipe *their* partner.

The study also asked people about their personality types. You could take an educated guess; poachers score highly on being unconscientious, outgoing, selfish, unempathic and talkative. They major in self-disclosure, especially about sex.

Those who are successfully poached also score more highly on being outgoing and liking to talk about sex. The talking is clearly a prelude to having it. As you might expect, attractive, self-confident people are better at poaching. It's not clear if poaching is age-related, since all the studies are carried out on young adults.

Although no one likes poaching, there's a lot of it about. Maybe if the woman you are trying to poach says yes then you deserve each other. The studies showed that the poacher and the poached both scored highly on unfaithfulness.

OFFICE ROMANCE

I've been friends with a new guy at work for a few months. I thought he was gorgeous and now he's said he's very attracted to me. I'd really like to start seeing him – we are both nearly thirty – but we work in the same department and I like my job too. Is it a mistake to have a relationship with someone you work with?

He's not your boss – which is good. But you get points deducted for working in the same department. There's a risk of competition between you, and being an item within a team can be claustrophobic. You are sensible, if not sufficiently blinded by love, to see the potential for disaster. Grim indeed to sit in meetings with a still steaming ex. But let's be practical: you have to meet Mr Right or Wrong somewhere.

Around 8 out of 10 people in the UK have workplace romances, according to a survey of 1,274 employees by the law firm Peninsula. This and other surveys show that 6 out of 10 of us have at least one long-term relationship (including marriage) with people we meet at work.

You're more likely to meet your future partner at work than pretty much anywhere else. It's partly an exposure thing – both in terms of time and proximity. A survey in *Psychology Today* says that one third of work romances are between people in the same or adjoining offices. Apparently we're too lazy to check out the talent downstairs.

Your workplace has already done the screening work of a dating agency – combining people who share ambitions and interests and often cultural values. You may learn more about someone by working with them than going out on any number of dates. Working closely together builds familiarity, intimacy and trust. These don't sound sexy, but strangely they are. Work itself can be arousing – all those deadlines and anxiety, all those late-into-the-evening sessions and bonding in the pub afterwards. And who better to understand the pressure of your work than the person sitting at the desk behind you?

Dr Lisa Mainiero, professor of management at the Fairfield University School of Management, surveyed over 100 female executives in the US to determine the characteristics of those relationships that worked. Those most likely to succeed are between peers from different departments. Couples should agree how they'll behave at work (no snogging, fighting or blabbing about their relationship) and what they will do if they split up (be professional). Remember, the odds are that most office romances will split up, so at least try to think it through. While two thirds of office romances start in secret, Mainiero's research shows that those you work with invariably guess and that it's the serious relationships that quickly go public. Most people will be happy for you – everyone loves a lover. But around one third of office romances are between people already in other relationships – these really aren't popular at all.

So as long as he isn't too distracting and you don't tell your mates at work about either your rows or your unbelievable sex, you should be fine. Ideally he'd get a job in another department. Not too far away, though, or he might get interested in someone else.

ONE NIGHT ONLY

I met this guy at a friend's wedding four weeks ago and we had a fantastic time dancing and drinking together. We had sex that night and although in the morning he said he'd ring, he hasn't. I hadn't meant it to be a one-night stand. Do you think the fact we had sex so quickly has put him off?

You could always ring and ask him. Sex on the first date doesn't preclude a lifetime of happiness together. But if you're asking whether it's a good idea to have sex on the first date, the answer is no. Unless there are bombs falling and you don't think there will be a tomorrow.

This hard-line approach is for self-preservation, because sex on the first date is usually influenced by one of the three

D's: drink, drugs or desperation. Sex is not a fast track to cementing a relationship, and unless you have a PhD in sexual pleasuring you won't increase your desirability as a partner by having sex with someone you've known for only a few hours. It is rarely satisfying sexually and can be embarrassing afterwards.

A one-night stand has the expectation that the relationship will end before noon the next day. Such sex without strings has to be okay if you both agreed – but people don't have that chat first. Hence the ambiguity the morning after. An *Observer*/ICM poll of 1,000 Britons last year found that more than half had had a one-night stand, but other surveys range from 10 to 50 per cent. If there's a perception that everyone is having sex with each other immediately, the reality is different. A MORI poll of 1,790 adults showed most waited one to three weeks before having sex with their current partner. According to the same poll only 1 in 10 men and 3 per cent of women had sex on the first date.

Would you have regretted not having sex with him? A study from Arizona State University on lifetime regrets of 120 men and women showed that vastly more men than women regretted not 'trying harder to sleep with' someone. Women had an even mixture of regrets about who they had and hadn't had sex with. This may be because some women, you included, consider sex to be more than a recreational activity.

That's not to say it can't be a recreational activity, but public opinion is still against the idea. A recent Sheffield University study of forty-six women aged between twenty and eighty-three by Dr Sharon Hinchliff found that 90 per cent thought casual sex was wrong and done out of neediness rather than sexual liberation. Some younger women were harsher than older ones, and only 10 per cent of all the women admitted to having had one-night stands themselves. Those who had had one disapproved as much as those who hadn't. Men's attitudes are likely to be less harsh. Another study of public opinion comes from a questionnaire survey from Texas Tech University in the journal *Personal Relationships*. This study, of 148 men and 148 women, found that while women and men thought less of people who had sex on a first date, they thought equally badly of men and women. Which has to be progress of sorts.

So there still seems to be a stigma about the one-night stand that *Sex in the City* hasn't dispelled. However, this doesn't mean your guy should think any less of you – he was there too.

TALL STORY

I am short (5 ft 1 in) and my husband is 6 ft 1 in. I have never been attracted to small men although we'd make a more normal-looking couple. Someone told me it's because short women need tall men to have children of average size. Is this why I fell for him?

I'm sure there's more to your husband than his height, but studies show that generally women prefer taller men and that men prefer smaller women. In 2000 the UK's National Child Development Study analysed data from 10,000 people born in a single week in March 1958. The taller the men were (above the average of 5 ft 10 ins), the more likely they were to be married with children. Women were most likely to be married and have children if they were below average height (between 4 ft 9 ins and 5 ft 1 in) – the average is around 5 ft 4 ins. The study's authors are not sure why men prefer short women, but in evolutionary terms tall women are seen as less fertile because they tend to reach puberty later than shorter women. However, there's no evidence that taller women conceive less quickly or less often than shorter women today, so perhaps preferences could also evolve a little.

Many studies show that women find taller men more attractive. Tall, dark and handsome men to be precise. They correlate height with health, wealth and status, which is pretty accurate. Research does show a basic link between social deprivation and height – unfortunately for shorter men. A study of 3,200 Polish men found unmarried and childless men were an inch shorter than those who were married with children. Women were found actively to select taller men, although it wasn't height that won them over but the desirable qualities they inferred from it. And women are not alone in believing taller men are better. American studies show the belief that taller is better for men is a genuine widespread phenomenon: there's evidence that taller men are more likely to be selected for jobs, chosen for promotion and if, they're politicians, voted for by the electorate.

Surely there's some evidence that we're not as shallow as this suggests? Studies of lonely hearts advertisements show that 80 per cent of women who requested meeting men of a certain height wanted someone over 6 ft tall, and almost all of them wanted a man who was at least four inches taller than they were. However, once on dates common sense trumps evolution and they're more likely to rate other factors such as personality and intelligence as just as important as height.

Genetic studies suggest a link between the heights of mother and son and of father and daughter. The authors of the UK National Child Development Study say that taller fathers have taller daughters. In your case this would bring any daughter you had up to an average height. Even so, it's less the height adjustment for your kids that made you marry him and more what you thought being tall represented. Let's hope he delivers on both counts.

DUMB CHOICE

I'm a thirty-year-old single woman and I have no trouble finding dates. However, they rarely progress beyond the first date and I get the feeling I am intimidating men. A friend recommended I act 'stupid' on dates because men don't like women who appear to be more intelligent, confident and attractive than them. Is my friend right?

As a strategy, 'acting stupid' has limitations. When do you plan to reveal the real you? Evolutionary psychologists say that men want women who are great at child-bearing (so men should look at teeth and muscle tone) and that women like men with fat wallets (so check the inside pocket). Can it be that we haven't moved with the times at all? A survey in *Sex Roles* of 199 people in the Netherlands (specifically Amsterdam), showed only a minority interest in the intelligence of a future mate. Physical attractiveness, and being honest, reliable and fun to be with came out top for both sexes. Men cared more about looks than women. There are many studies that replicate these findings. However, women may overestimate the extent to which men are intimidated by intelligent women. A match. com survey found that while most men said they'd be happy to marry a career-minded woman (who one assumes would be intelligent), most women thought it would put men off.

Anecdotally, men say they want women who are almost as smart as them (the 'almost' is of critical importance). There are, however, no anecdotes suggesting men want someone less attractive. But how attractive is a woman with a high IQ?

A study led by Michelle Taylor from the University of Edinburgh, in the journal *Personality and Individual Differences*, compared the IQ tests of 900 people taken at age eleven with their marriageable status forty years later. For every 16-point rise in IQ, women were 40 per cent less likely to be married. When it appeared in the media, women shuddered. But this is an association which could mean women know marriage benefits men more than women and decided not to get married, or it may mean their chances are reduced because they do intimidate some men. The truth is probably a bit of both, and on balance the studies from America show women with high-powered jobs are no less likely to be married than other women. Heather Boushey, an economist at the Center for Economic and Policy Research in Washington, DC, found that out of women between the ages of thirty to forty-four who earn more than $100,000 a year, 88 per cent are married, compared with 82 per cent of other women of the same age.

If marriage prospects are similar, what about the likelihood of divorce? It used to be thought that women who were college graduates were more likely to divorce, perhaps because they could be financially independent afterwards. But more recent research, including a study from the University of Maryland looking at 16,000 marriages between 1990 and 1994 shows that where a wife had a college education the chances of divorce in the first ten years were 16.5 per cent compared with 38 per cent when the wife did not have further education.

Being too opinionated, not listening or seeming uninterested in your date will put men off. Being over-confident is also unattractive. Dates may make you anxious and more intimidating than you either realize or mean to be. These are more likely to scare men off than your intelligence. Relax and play nice rather than dumb.

FIRST MOVER

I really like this guy who is the friend of a friend of mine. I've met him a few times. We see each other at parties and talk to each other, but nothing has ever come of it. I know he is single, so if he liked me he would have done something about it by now. So shall I leave it or try to find out if he is interested?

It should be easy to know if someone is interested in you, but it isn't. All this platonic mateship makes for a blurring of boundaries between friendships and relationships. It's possible to go on a date without knowing it. But even in times of strict dating convention there were still ambiguities. Jane Austen's novels often revolve around questions of 'Does he (insert name of uptight romantic hero) fancy me or not?'

It's highly possible for people to misconstrue romantic intentions, and conventions are meant to help. Going up to someone in a bar and asking them if they'd like a drink is a recognized sign of interest. Other more subtle ones, such as him leaning towards you, engaging you in exclusive conversation and locking eyes with you are harder to gauge. He may just be strange or intense. Studies show an overlap between many of the qualities people look for in their friends with those that they want in potential partners. They may not be sure themselves which way it will go until they know each other better. Conversely, some people (and they may be the lucky ones) construe more interest from people they meet than actually exists.

You don't know if your guy is interested or not. Men are still expected to make the first move, but not all of them do it all of the time, and he may think you won't be interested. Maybe he can't tell that you like him more than anyone else in your group of friends because you haven't given him any reason to hope. No one likes rejection, and it's awkward to ask someone out and see the horror in their face. There's a sweet academic study involving 522 people called 'Who's Going to Make the First Move? Pluralistic Ignorance as an Impediment to Relationship Formation' in the *Journal of Social and Personal Relationships*. 'Pluralistic ignorance' refers to how people see someone behaving like them (i.e. not asking them out) but infer they're doing so for different reasons. So neither of you is making a move but although you're attracted to him, you assume he's not interested. This research looked at previous smaller studies and hypothetical scenarios, but the finding that self-protection can override romantic imperative seems fairly obvious, though it points to a rather feeble way to live your life.

Go-betweens like your friend can help (tell your friend you're interested) and you can try to assess (with others) whether he likes you. Try flirting with someone standing next to him and see if he flinches. Actually, don't. A far better idea is to be brave and ask him out for a drink. There's some evidence that it will be the lesser of two evils. Most people can get over rejection especially from someone they don't know that well, whereas a study of what people regret most from the University of Cornell found that one of the most common regrets people had in their lives was missing a romantic opportunity.

WISH YOU WERE HERE

I'm going on holiday with friends, and I'm keen to meet someone as I've been single for a while. But when I've had holiday romances in the past they've been disastrous. Why does this happen – are holiday romances doomed?

Holiday romances are not known for their longevity. What can it be about sun, bare flesh, a litre of something you'd never drink at home and a week of lie-ins that promotes romance or, to be more cynical, casual sex? You need to be cautious about trying to start a long-term relationship on holiday, because normal rules of engagement are suspended.

If you meet someone at home maybe you'll start off by seeing each other a few times over the first couple of weeks. On holiday you can see each other all day, every day. You may not be able to avoid it. Suddenly this is the most intense relationship you've ever had and, what's more, it's so easy – you're both so open (and often so drunk) and so passionate. And it's so unrealistic. Real life is more mundane. There's no context to refer to when you see someone in swimwear at the pool bar.

Surveys by interested parties such as condom manufacturers, travel companies and doctors specializing in sexually transmitted diseases (was there really no room to pack the condoms?) show that between a fifth and a half of us have had holiday romances. Who knows how many people find the man or woman of their dreams (or even want to?). A Sky Travel survey of 2,000 people found only 1 in 10 holiday romances lasted longer than a week, but a Mori poll of 505 people put it closer to half, while an *Observer* poll found that 20 per cent became long-term relationships. It's hard to quantify, especially if you read the *Observer* but also use Sky Travel services.

Some people have no intention of embarking on anything serious. Researchers from St George's Hospital asked 150 people in the airport departure hall at Tenerife about sex on their holiday. Surprisingly they weren't told to get lost, and they found that 48 out of 136 people had had sex with someone other than their partner (but the holiday reps had offered champagne to the first new couple to have sex).

Sometimes the holiday romance is taken more seriously by one person than the other. In a study that asked thirty-five women about their holiday encounters, Michelle Thomas from Cardiff University found that although women often felt incredibly close to their new partner on holiday, their trust was sometimes misplaced. It was not uncommon, for example, for men not to mention their girlfriend at home until after they'd had sex. Thomas warns that time becomes compressed on holiday and caution is thrown to the wind.

Why you shouldn't follow suit is that you want this to be for real. Many holiday romances are casual because people want them to fade before their tan does. Most people have holiday romances with people from their country – it's more convenient. There are people who fall in love with locals and never go home, but you'd have to guess, not many. No one can help you with the choosing; but the bars of Tenerife and Ibiza are not full of people looking for commitment. If you do meet someone, take it steady, and be clear that you are looking for something longer than a week. Don't spend all your time with him: you're holidaying with friends. Don't dilute your judgement with too much alcohol and don't intensify the relationship. Follow a more 'at home' trajectory. If you do make it home, do the dating thing rather than assume you've been catapulted into the status of established couple. And don't take too many photos – it's tempting fate.

EX OR HEX?

One of my best friends broke up with her boyfriend four months ago. I always thought he was gorgeous, and when I saw him recently we talked all evening and had a goodnight kiss. He said he wanted to see me again. Their split was mutual. Shall I ask my friend if it's okay to see him or forget about him?

'All's fair in love and war' is one way of looking at things; another is 'Thou shalt not date your friend's ex'. Find out your friend's view before you proceed, or risk losing her for ever. It's unsettling to think of a friend sleeping with your ex, however mutual the split was or however average the sex. These sorts of relationships are referred to as a form of recycling (celebrities are forever going out with friends' exe's) or even by the horrible term 'sloppy seconds'. There's an implication that the subsequent partner is second best. Yet the likelihood of being attracted to a friend's partner is fairly high. Friends are usually like us in terms of their age, education, what they earn and how attractive they are, and people tend to be attracted to people who are similar to them. So you're more likely to be similar to your friend's partner than a stranger in a club. You'll also know them better, having been out with them socially and heard intimate details from your friend. It's good manners to ignore any attraction, but there's an inevitable sexual rivalry between friends when it comes to finding lovers.

Studies (mostly of undergraduates, who may be more susceptible to this) show that nearly 1 in 5 men and 29 per cent of women have flirted with a friend's partner and that over half have competed with a friend to attract a potential partner. In a study of young people carried out by researchers at the University of Texas, forty-eight men and sixty-nine women were asked to rank the costs and benefits of their (same-sex) friends. Out of ten costs, of which cruelty was sadly top, stealing of boyfriends or girlfriends came fifth. Perhaps the two costs are related.

In another study, of 406 college students from universities in the south and southwest of the US published in *Personal Relationships*, 67 per cent of people said they were the victim of 'intrasexual rivalry' from a friend, although they may have used different words to describe it.

This is not to say you have poached your friend's ex yet, but if stealing a boyfriend is disloyalty as an art form, dating them even after the relationship is over is not going to delight your friend. Some friends and even the ex partner will take a 'waste not, want not' view. Your friend may, however, wonder if you always lusted after her partner, making the conversations you may have had about the relationship dishonest and self-interested on your part.

I could find no research on whether these relationships last. You're likely to be similar (that's good), but your friends may not like it (which is bad). Out of courtesy, ask your friend if it's okay, but 'It's absolutely fine' is unlikely to mean that. Expect your friendship to change (not for the better), and so only do this if you think the romance is worth it. And remember, your friend won't want to hear the intimate details.

UNSETTLING THOUGHTS

After a two-year failed relationship I came to London from Germany to pursue my artistic ambitions. I also wanted to enjoy 'exploring' men and relationships but am involved with someone I care for but who has no goals or ambitions. I feel disappointed in him and am dating other men – and have told him. If I really loved him, would I do this? At forty-one should I stop making excuses for not being in a stable relationship and settle down? Should I judge men by another set of values and not by their standing in life?

In your question you're really asking yourself what to do. Which is a relief because you're the person best placed to know.

Everyone settles for someone to some degree. Otherwise we'd all have rich, beautiful, exciting yet trustworthy partners – the type the research says we want. Some would argue it's better to be single than settle for less than ideal, but that depends on how realistic you are. When you ask people more specifically about long-term relationships, people want partners who are faithful and good companions – which sounds like a dog, until you get to the third requirement which is for good sex. These characteristics scored highest in an Australian survey of 1,200 people (the Relationships Indicators Survey) and 2,020 Americans (the Pew Survey). A partner's standing in life wasn't mentioned.

The importance of compatibility, however, was raised (by 1 in 10 of the Australian survey), and ambitious people like you might struggle to commit to someone who seems 'goal-less'. If he disappoints you now, the natural history of relationships suggests he won't delight you later.

If you want to settle, there's good evidence for the characteristics to look for. One plus One is a British organization that researches and educates people about all sorts of relationships. In their report 'Biographical Determinations of Marital Quality' they looked at the relationships of over 10,000 people and found positive associations for someone your family and friends approve of, who's well educated, quite well off, communicative, conscientious and secure and whose parents did not divorce in a blaze of acrimony. If the person is also happy in their job, copes well with stress and is healthy, then you won't be settling but winning the lottery.

The average age for marrying has gone up in the developed world in the past few decades from twenty-seven and a half for men and twenty-five and a half for women to nearly thirty-two for men and twenty-nine and a half for women in 2001; and there's some evidence that settling later is better, so if you don't want children, don't rush. You may, however, have heard of the demographic study 'Marriage Patterns in the United States', which was reported in 1986 in *Newsweek* as finding that 'a single forty-year-old woman has a better chance of being killed by a terrorist than getting married (a 2.6 per cent chance).' It wasn't true: other researchers were quick to re-calculate the chance of getting married as up to 23 per cent, and others have since said it's even higher. I'd suggest you explore what you want first before you explore any other men.

REBOUND TO FAIL?

I've met this guy who I really like but four months ago he came out of a long-term relationship (he says it was a mutual decision). I'm worried that he'll use me as a 'transitional' person to get over his relationship and then move on. How can I tell if it's for real or if he's on the rebound?

You're worried about being used and dumped, which can happen in any relationship. But there's something about a rebounding lover that strikes fear into any heart that's still beating. Dr Gilda Carle, author of *Don't Bet on the Prince: How to Have the Man You Want by Betting on Yourself*, is unsurprisingly (given her book title) not a fan of rebound relationships. She warns not to get involved with anyone less than nine months after they've come out of a serious relationship. The perceived wisdom is that rebounders need to grieve and work out why their last relationship unravelled. This assumes people learn from their previous relationships rather than just go out with their mates for a few drinks. Another way of looking at things is expressed in the old saying, 'The best way to get over a man is to get under the next one'. The website rebound-relationships.com says that rebound relationships can be unrealistically fast paced, with the rebounder moving on to a 'proper relationship' surprisingly quickly. Tips for spotting a rebounder include their persistent snivelling over their ex, an unrealistically speedy attachment to you (proposing can be an extreme variant) and neediness or bitterness towards the opposite sex.

Along with this largely anecdotal evidence comes some research from Nicholas H. Wolfinger, a demographer (who told me this makes him agnostic about what's in people's heads – he does the counting not the psychoanalysis) from the University of Utah. His study of 1,171 adults in the National Survey of Families and Households found that as far as marriage or living together (and then going on to marry) were concerned there was no rebound effect. Couples who rushed into second marriages were no more likely to split up than those who waited longer. Second marriages are more likely to end than first ones, but how quickly people rush into them doesn't seem to effect their longevity. Wolfinger says he couldn't look at dating because there isn't the data.

In Britain, John Ermisch of the Institute for Social and Economic Research found in his analysis that one half of people who leave a cohabiting relationship and 30 per cent of divorced people find new partners within two years. The study doesn't say much about emotional recovery, but Judith Wallerstein's research estimated that it took women three years to feel stable after a marriage split up, while men were feeling much better after an average of two years. However, her study was carried out in the 1980s, and as divorce has become more common, recovery may be quicker. Wolfinger believes that people vary in how quickly they recover from divorce. Most of the upheaval, such as moving, takes place in the first year of splitting up, and some people need to feel settled before they can start dating again.

Common sense suggests you take things at a normal, non-rebound pace; don't expect him to feel nothing for his ex but it's reasonable that he shouldn't see her. You may need to be supportive but maintain some distance and an independent social life. If he's got any sense he'll reassure you that it's you he wants to be with.

After the First Few Dates

CAN'T HURRY LOVE

I'm thirty-seven and have been seeing a man who is nothing like my previous boyfriends. He is loving, thoughtful and clever. Usually I go for action men and lust. This didn't start like that. I enjoy having sex with him and think I love him. But for a long-term relationship shouldn't I be in love with him? Can I make myself fall in love with him?

For long-term relationships the script usually requires that you should be *in* love. But psychology researchers and anyone with half a brain can work out that there are two types of love in relationships. The first is the romantic type that develops rapidly and becomes an obsession. You're either with them or thinking about being with them, all of the time. Passion is a prerequisite and obsession and jealousy frequent side effects. Then there's companionate (friendship-type) love that grows strongly with time and is driven by coming to know someone deeply – often in ways that nobody else knows (or would want to know). Guess which one's the better bedrock for an enduring relationship?

As president of the International Association for Relationship Research, Dr Robert Milardo knows quite a bit about love. He believes that falling in love is an intentional phenomenon, however magical it feels. You couldn't fall in love with just anyone; you have to find them attractive and share some values – you have to want to do it. We all focus, albeit unconsciously, on the aspects we find most attractive in a person, even as we're falling.

You're quite clear that it's been about lust before, and you like the fact this man offers more. What worries you is that he didn't offer up the lust first. Each year Milardo asks his twenty-eight students in relationships studies whether it's best to start off with romantic or friendship-type love in a relationship. This year nearly all of them said having friendship first gave the relationship a more solid basis. A broader survey of over 200 engaged US men and women in their twenties found that three quarters rejected the definition of their relationship as being 'head over heels in love'.

I'm afraid there are no meaningful statistics to help you. There are no studies on falling in love with someone because you want to. No one would sign up for a randomized controlled trial that assigned you a lover on the throw of a coin. All the studies can tell you is that it's companionate and not passionate love that makes for intimate and sound relationships. They're not mutually exclusive and either can come first. Everyone knows couples who started off as friends and then fell in love.

Statistics aside, academics can't even agree on what love is – an emotion or, as one research paper put it, 'a goal-orientated motivational state'. Arguments rage over whether there is a facial expression for love (as there is for joy or sorrow). Surveys of ordinary folk show they do rate love as an emotion – in particular they say it makes them happy to think about the person they love. Being in love generally includes sexual desire (you like having sex with him) and feeling good about yourself.

There are studies of arranged marriages, but they wouldn't help you – the religious and cultural differences make the results inapplicable. After all, you are able to choose. I'd suggest you choose someone you want to do the business of loving and living with.

FRIENDLY FIRE

My friends don't like my boyfriend. Some knew him from university, where he had a reputation of being unfaithful to his girlfriends, but that was three years ago. They make excuses about why they can't meet us and keep asking me why I'm with him. I don't feel we can go out together with my friends as they seem so hostile. What should I do?

Any man who has been unfaithful to girlfriends (I note the plural) will not score highly with your friends. For while friends can get jealous when you start a relationship (worrying you'll have less time for them) they mostly want you to be happy. They either fear he won't make you happy or dislike him for other reasons. In your case it's clearer than most why they might dislike him.

No relationship is an island; it's surrounded by friends and family all of whom have something to say about it. Unfortunately, most research focuses on how couples develop their relationship in isolation, rather than seeing how their social network affects them. One study in the *Journal of Personality and Social Psychology* in 1972 discovered a Romeo and Juliet effect (a term applied to many relationship issues by researchers), where parents who disapproved and interfered with the relationship made it stronger. Other studies have not replicated these historical findings and instead show that it's parental approval that nourishes relationships (how conventional we've become).

This is shown in a more recent study of 101 dating couples at Illinois University. If you are not twenty, middle class and attending a university in the Midwest then be cautious in applying the results to your own life – but as you'll see, the conclusions are more common sense than wildly radical. The study found that both men and women felt happier and were more committed to each other when their friends approved of their relationship. When friends tell a couple they're a good match and how much they enjoy going out with them, that couple start believing they really are a couple. What's more they'll think they make a good couple. And when friends say, 'He's a great guy really, he didn't mean to throw up on you,' it makes you less likely to dump him. Friends (women in particular) can either support or trash relationships by adding information into the mix when they're analysing the relationship. Which they do continuously. Although in this study, where couples were young, many of them didn't last long anyway. When a couple stays together for a while their groups of friends start to overlap and this strengthens the relationship.

So if you're happy in your relationship and think your boyfriend is a reformed character, you need to raise the issue with your friends and, if need be, stand up for him. Are they being overprotective because of rumours, or do they dislike him for who he is now? Do they think he's boring? Do they think he treats you badly (you might want to look at that too)? You may have to reconcile yourself to seeing your friends without him. But don't alienate your friends, because if he does turn out to be a philandering scumbag you'll really need them.

ROUND THE BEND

My girlfriend is a terrible driver, and every time we go on trips together we have huge arguments that can end up with her pulling over and stopping. When I drive she'll criticize my driving too. Do most couples do this, why do they do it, and how can we stop?

Cars are small, confined spaces, which make them ideal to fight in. Asking why couples argue in a car is like asking why childbirth is painful. It's part of the human condition. Arguments accelerate in a car faster than you can go from 0 to 30 mph, and unless you pull over there's no escape.

A 2007 ICM poll of 2,071 drivers over eighteen years of age for the online motoring site MissMotors.co.uk found that 1 in 10 (really so few?) will be arguing with their partner within fifteen minutes of starting their car journey. About 40 per cent of the arguments are caused by men criticizing their partner's driving. Just over 1 in 10 are caused by men taking control of the car stereo. (After a bitter radio custody battle my partner once pulled off the volume knob; oh, how we laughed.) But this antipathy from men is not limited to who's in the car with them – they'll argue with anyone on the road. The survey also found that while almost all women had lost their temper while driving, it was overwhelmingly with male drivers.

Since men and women are essentially arguing over who's the best driver, what does the research show? In 2001 the Advertising Standards Authority ruled that an insurance company could advertise cheaper car insurance for women because they 'are better drivers' (the measure being involvement in fewer accidents). The Social Issues Research Centre (SIRC) has published a report on sex differences in driving, citing evidence that men (especially those under twenty-five) are more aggressive drivers, more likely to speed, take risks and crash (a 1992 study showed twice the rate for men as for women). Poor men: the SIRC says they carry round a larger 'interpersonal bubble', and when someone goes near it they can get road rage. Home Office statistics also show that 94 per cent of those convicted of causing death by dangerous driving are men. A classic accident for men is taking a bend too fast.

Women, however, are more likely to be involved in more minor accidents, what could be passed off as 'errors of judgement'. Their accidents are caused by pulling out of junctions, reversing into skips or misjudging how close the car is that's behind them. But as Professor Frank McKenna of

Reading University once told a transport conference, 'precious few people die parking'. Other research, from Johns Hopkins University, argues that women drive less than men and that this may account for them having an overall lower rate of crashes.

At least disputes about map reading can now be solved by satellite navigation. Research shows that most arguments are best resolved by humour and compromise rather than sulking. You can stop arguing by not getting in the same car. Criticizing your partner's driving is going to cause a fight, so you'll have to exercise self-control and stop doing it. But if you must drive together, the American Automobile Association warns that distracting the driver causes up to half of accidents. However, you're more likely to crash looking at scenery or nodding off, so arguing may not be so bad after all.

SPLIT THE DIFFERENCE?

About two years ago I found new happiness with a lovely divorced man with two teenagers. While acknowledging the value of the connection he suddenly withdrew, saying he couldn't commit and admitting cowardice, while insisting he is happy as a bachelor. It seems so sad – I truly have yet to meet a nicer man. Is he just afraid, or is this a polite way of breaking it off after a few months of mutual enjoyment?

If he says he is breaking it off because he can't commit and is a coward, you'll have to believe him. The alternative is to accuse him of lying to save your feelings and insist that he tells you he doesn't like you enough (even if it's not true). Either way, it's over, and his reason sounds sufficiently honest to be genuine. If there's anything left to understand it's probably that some people don't want to commit to close relationships after they've got divorced. Many studies show that while women have most stress during a divorce, men have it later and for longer and are more likely to smoke, drink, throw themselves into work and engage in 'frantic sexual activity', as one study so nicely puts it, in attempts to get over it. Men often mourn the loss of their children and home more than their wives. However, the research isn't consistent, with some studies showing little difference in how men and women cope with divorce. Having friends and family to talk to is helpful for both sexes as long as they don't tell you where you went wrong.

Your nice man may have had such a bad experience of marriage that he's become cynical and less willing to commit. Maybe he never had the support he needed to cope with his divorce. Perhaps he also knows that bringing children (especially teenagers) into any new relationship increases the chances of the relationship ending in everyone's tears. Maybe he understands the responsibilities and risks of commitment and doesn't want them – even with someone he enjoyed being with as much as you.

Of course, many divorced people do have further committed relationships. A study by the Institute of Social and Economic Research using data from the British Household Panel Survey found that 43 per cent of divorced people will have another partner within five years, a lower percentage than people who split up after living together. This is partly because people who are living together are on average younger. Men are twice as likely to remarry as women.

But as these statistics are population-based they can't tell you anything about your man. A study of 208 divorced people published in the *Journal of Marriage and Family* showed that people found it harder to get over a divorce if they were older and hadn't wanted one and did better if they had a new relationship. You should stop torturing yourself over what he really meant and accept what he is saying. He is a nice man, you had a good time, but he prefers being single. You, however, would prefer not to be single, so you need to keep looking. Don't get hung up on him being the one, because without wishing to sound unromantic (or confusing), there's more than one right one for everyone.

ROMEO AND JULIET

I've been having a relationship with a girl who I knew at college. We have mutual friends and kept it secret in case it didn't work out. Now that we're being more open about our relationship she's rapidly lost interest in me. Would this have happened if we'd still kept our relationship secret, or does it show she wasn't really interested?

The trouble with secret relationships is that it's hard to know how interested either of you really is. Secret relationships feel hot because the secrecy increases the excitement. They are the stuff of plays (*Romeo and Juliet*). But do they make people happy? Not in plays, where lovers end up drinking poison, and nor do they in real life, because secrecy gets in the way of building a commitment. People sometimes hide relationships (as they do early pregnancies) until they think they're viable. Workplace romances, affairs with married people, inter-religious or gay relationships may be hidden for longer out of fear that colleagues, family or friends may disapprove. The rationale that a couple will be less embarrassed if it doesn't work out if no one knew about it in the first place is somewhat misguided. Once a secret relationship is over, everyone knows.

The corrosive rather than enhancing effect of secrecy (you might think sharing a secret brings people closer) is shown in a study from the University of Georgia published in *Personal Relationships*. Researchers asked 201 women and thirty-nine men aged between sixteen and thirty-nine who were in relationships if they were keeping them secret and, if so, how much pressure that created. They also asked them how upset they'd be if the relationship ended. Of the thirty-five who had secret relationships, most said they'd be less upset and they were also more likely to feel their relationship was a burden.

A further study by the same research team of forty-six people in secret relationships found that compared to people in public relationships they were less satisfied with their partners and rated their relationships as poorer. The quality of secret relationships falls quickly because after the initial excitement it's too much like hard work. Most people in secret relationships get fed up of lying to friends about why they're not around some weekends and of reassuring their family that being single is great. There's also the problem of secrecy being a barrier to couples getting close; in a secret relationship you can't talk to other people about how you feel and get support for the relationship. You can't even cuddle each other in public. By not going public you can't acknowledge to the world that the other person is special to you. And since relationships are about being special to someone else, this means that secret relationships have a serious design flaw.

Secrecy may be intense, but it denies a couple the fun of early relationships and the opportunity to get to know each other. It can be hard to know what's most interesting, the person or the secrecy. Going public is often a turning point. It's not unusual to find that once the secrecy's gone there isn't much left.

POLES APART

Do opposites attract? My girlfriend loves travelling and opera and has political leanings to the right. Travelling is okay; I hate opera, and have always been politically to the left. We get on really well, but do these differences matter longer term?

Only when you're dealing with magnetic poles do opposites attract. Relationship research would say it's conclusively proven that like attracts like. The term 'assortative mating' refers to the idea that there's a systematic pattern in how people choose partners (and mostly they seem to pick people like them). In measuring this phenomenon most research has rated the characteristics of one partner against the other's. It's found that couples usually share religious and political beliefs and are about the same age. They are fairly similar in their education, intelligence and what they think matters in life. Most people go for someone as good-looking or plain as they are (excluding rich people who of course are all gorgeous). Part of the explanation for who we choose lies in who we meet. At work, at your gym, at a friend's party, you'll meet people quite like you.

You may, however, also be familiar with the saying 'love is blind', suggesting you can fall for anyone, should you get the chance to meet them. But psychologists argue it's temporary: after three months you can see again and usually go off them. There's a strong drive to see similarities in someone you're attracted to even when they don't exist. A small, not very scientific study from the University of Maine in the 1980s asked sixty men to rank on a questionnaire how similar a woman was to them. Those that found her attractive were nearly twice as likely to find her remarkably similar to themselves as those who didn't. Another study from the University of Notre Dame in *Personal Relationships* asked 301 college students who were in relationships (people were recruited as couples into the study; their mean age was around twenty) how similar they were to their other half. They asked about people's ability to be emotionally close to others, how secure they felt and how much they felt their partner understood them. The study showed that couples who felt the closest to each other were most likely to think their partner was just like them – even when they scored quite differently on the psychological tests.

If you differ in some areas, even religion, you may still have a great relationship. Why your differences may not matter may be down to your personalities. A study from Iowa University of 291 newly wed couples in the *Journal of Personality and Social Psychology* who had dated for three and a half years found that in a committed relationship it was similarities in personalities (such as how open or caring someone is) that kept couples happy and helped them negotiate their differences, for example what music they preferred to have on in the car. Usually couples seem to hook up on the basis of quite skin-deep similarities and see if it works out afterwards. You, on the other hand, may have chosen more wisely, and it's the similarities in your personalities that will bring you long-term happiness.

CONTROLLING THE REMOTE

My boyfriend and I have blazing rows over who's got the remote control when we watch television. It drives me mad that he flicks through programmes all the time and insists on holding on to it all evening. Friends of mine say their boyfriends do this too. Is it a man thing, and what's the best way to encourage sharing of the remote?

The TV remote has attracted much attention from sociologists, psychologists and media researchers. What looks like a functional piece of plastic has been studied as a modern extension of the male role of hunter-gatherer and as a potent symbol of female oppression – with batteries. An early study in 1986 by David Morley looked at the viewing habits of eighteen working-class and lower middle-class families in London. He found that men were more likely than women to plan what they were going to watch in the evening and that their tight grip on the remote control was symbolic of their control over the choice of programmes. Women often complained that their husbands would change channels without asking, something they rarely did themselves. Morley was sure that these findings would not be replicated in the middle classes, but in fact he was wrong. A YouGov poll of 4,118 adults in 2004 found that the majority felt a man (usually a dad) still ruled the remote control. Researchers have been interested in whether control over the remote represents control over the rest of a couple's relationship. You may have worked this out already. Anecdotally there are stories of men sneaking remotes into their pockets if they have to leave the room. Does this oppression know no bounds? In 1993 an American journalist called Ellen Goodman went as far as to call the remote 'the most reactionary implement currently used to undermine equality in modern marriage'.

Perhaps men just find it comforting to have the control near them. A survey of thirty-six people in the *Journal of Marriage and Family* found that men most commonly had the remote on the seat or arm of their chair. This allowed them to do things with it that irritated their partners. Women were more likely than men to complain about channel surfing and a partner not turning back quickly enough after switching during a commercial break. Only a third of couples shared the remote.

Surveys show clear differences in the television viewing preferred by men and women; although who hasn't seen their man sneakily watch the odd makeover programme? Women traditionally prefer soap operas while men go for factual programmes. Women will often talk or do something useful while watching television; men are more likely to watch in concentrated silence.

If your relationship is otherwise happy you should be able to negotiate the remote control issue. Removing the batteries is only a temporary solution, buying another television is admitting defeat, splitting up even more so. Agree on what you both want to watch and on no one changing channels until either of you have asked first. You can buy remote blockers, but he's likely to run off with that too.

SEX AND LIES

My boyfriend has had sex with fewer people than I have. We've been together for two months and I've underplayed how many men I've slept with (it's sixteen and he's only mentioned six women), because I don't expect him to be thrilled. If he asks me outright I'll say eight, but he might find there were more. What should I do?

You could argue that your boyfriend should know who you've slept with, because to love you he should love your past. But I wouldn't argue that. I'm more of the persuasion that says, 'Why rub his nose in it?' This is because knowing your partner's entire sexual history, unless it's relevant (as in you've never had sex or you've been abused), will not enhance your relationship. You should still be honest about the sex you've had – just don't be an accountant about it. If arithmetical discrepancies come up later you can either show surprise that he's forgotten what you told him or tell him that it's in the past and none of his business.

If you go for an underestimate you won't be alone. Statisticians say that the average number of sexual partners men and women have (in a population) should be similar. Yet men frequently say they have two to four times as many sexual partners as women do. Men are more likely than women to visit prostitutes (who usually don't volunteer for sexual surveys and may have, according to a paper in the Proceedings of the National Academy of Sciences, over 600 partners a year) but researchers are divided over whether this can explain the maths. An *Observer* poll of 1,027 adults in 2002 produced an average of seven partners for women and 13 for men. A survey in 2005 by the University of Alberta of 2,065 heterosexual women and men came up with 8.6 for women and 31.9 for men. The Alberta researchers suggest that when stating how many partners they've had men roughly estimate (which means overestimate) while women count carefully (and forget some).

Women may also still feel the chill of a double standard. They are certainly less likely than men to boast about the number of sexual partners and more likely to 'forget' meaningless or particularly bad sex. Women generally do not want to be thought of as promiscuous. To test this hypothesis researchers from the University of Maine did a rather devious experiment. They divided 201 college students up into various groups, telling one group that the results of the sexual survey they were doing would be anonymous and a second that the researcher might have a look; a third group had electrodes attached to them and were told they were hooked up to a lie detector. Women who thought their answers were anonymous gave an average of 2.6 partners; those who thought their responses might be read said 3.4; while the poor women attached to the lie detector admitted to 4.4 partners. Men's answers hardly varied.

Your sexual past is indeed part of who you are – but most of us do some editing of our past. There has been research reported in *Psychology Today* saying that while men are happy to tell researchers how many women they've slept with, when it comes to telling their girlfriends they too forget some notches on their bedposts.

KISS OFF

My girlfriend said the other day that she didn't like how I kissed. It sounds stupid but it really upset me. We didn't really talk about it and I'm embarrassed to bring it up again. Is there much variation in kissing, and what do most people like?

As a teenager none of my friends wanted to kiss James (names have been changed to prevent the same hurt feelings that you have), because his tongue penetrated so far into your mouth that he made you gag and, worse, it was all wet and darted around like a snake. It's an oversight of nature that kissing, which exists in almost all cultures, is not an activity we're all naturally good at. Some of us suspect this and practice on mirrors or our own forearms from a young age. But kissing yourself is like trying to tickle yourself – it doesn't work. And who knows if what you're doing is pleasurable to someone else.

People do have opinions on kissing techniques. A study in *Evolutionary Psychology*, analysing answers from 162 men and 308 women who were psychology students at the University of Albany in New York, looked at various aspects of kissing, such as whether it increases sexual arousal (only if done well, you'd guess) and whether people use it to assess each other as relationship material. I'm not sure I go along with some of the hypotheses (can men really assess female fertility through what they taste when they're kissing – I think not), but since the results sound right, I'm prepared to. The researchers found that men generally preferred wetter kisses than women and enjoyed more tongue contact and open mouths. They preferred to slip their tongues in first – perhaps it's a territory thing. Men made more of a direct link between a kiss leading to sex, although some were happy to miss the kissing out altogether, with just over half saying they would have sex without kissing first. More women than men generally rated kissing as more important, both during sex and throughout relationships. They were also more interested in the state of their kissing partner's teeth than men were.

Kissing may not have the evolutionary significance that it used to as a way of tasting your partner and seeing how healthy they are (as the authors of the study suggest), but it's important that someone likes how you kiss. In a separate survey done by one of the authors, 58 men and 122 women were asked if they'd found someone attractive but been put off after kissing them. A total of 59 per cent of men and 66 per cent of women said yes. If you don't want to quiz your partner on how she likes being kissed you could, based on this study's findings, try less saliva and tongue penetration and a more relaxed, slower approach. In *Kissing*, by the kissing expert

Andrea Demirjian, she advises that the top tips for a good kiss are a clean mouth, a bit of anticipation, some sucking and biting of lips (theirs) and a relaxed tongue. To which I would add, not too wet and let them come up for air.

I WAS ONLY SAYING...

I come from a family where my parents never argued, but my girlfriend and I have quite a few arguments, often over little things. They are quite short-lived, although we shout at each other, and we generally get on well. Is your relationship better if you don't argue?

If a couple don't argue, it doesn't mean they have a great relationship. They may be uninterested in what their partner has to say. In which case what's there to argue about? This isn't to say your parents weren't happy but it is to say that arguing is not necessarily a barometer of how good or bad a relationship is. The research suggests that it's okay to argue if you do so in a civilized way. Conflict is normal in relationships; it's how you deal with it that determines how damaging it is.

Most couples when they argue do so over money, feeling jealous, who does the housework and communication ('You never talk to me, so let's argue about it') according to the UK research organization One Plus One. If you had children they would also be right up there as provoking arguments. And how often do couples argue about them? A survey of sixty couples (who had been seeing each other for at least five months) in the journal *Family Relations*, found that they argued on average nearly five times in two weeks. The arguments that made men most unhappy with their relationship were ones that came up again and again. The ones that made women unhappy were arguing over issues they felt never got sorted out. You can see the problem.

You may think having a civilized argument rather misses the point, but verbal weaponry can be immensely destructive. While sticks and stones may be needed to break bones, words can lay waste to your relationship. Researchers warn that contempt, sarcasm and aggression – the main ingredients of many fine arguments – are very hard to recover from. Name calling or anything that comes close to verbal abuse is a spectacularly bad idea. If you can, keep an argument at low intensity and try to negotiate. Avoid storing up ammunition in one row for use in future arguments or you will never get over anything, ever. Stick to the issue and do not drag in stuff you're still annoyed about from three years ago. Have some idea of what you want the outcome to be – don't just argue because there is nothing good on television. Couples who have serious problems will have arguments that are openly hostile and they'll be cruel to their partners. This type of arguing never makes a relationship better.

Quality arguments are ended either by someone saying sorry (forgiveness is a great healer of relationships, but you must feel it as well as say it) or by the couple mutually agreeing a solution. The most damaging are ended by one person stomping out or withdrawing emotionally. A study of seventy-nine married couples in the *Journal of Marriage and Family* found that men were most distressed when their partners withdrew from them after an argument, especially if they acted as if they didn't care about them any more (wandering off when their husband was trying to tell them about a bad day at work). Women were most upset when their husbands got angry and sarcastic.

The only way to never argue is to ignore any conflict, and most studies show that this doesn't make for happy relationships. You can be a happy couple and row; just do it with dignity, stick to the issue, say sorry afterwards and mean it.

What Happens Next?

GOING THE DISTANCE

I've been seeing an American guy for six months. His work is taking him home, and although we don't want to finish we're not at the 'let's stay together for ever' stage. We want to try to carry on our relationship even though it will be long distance. Is there any point, or will it just prolong the agony?

You shouldn't have a long-distance relationship just because you have the opportunity to do so. Only do it if you both want to commit to one. Your concern about potential agony is a worry because research shows that optimism in an LDR (as they're called) is an indicator of success. For this to work you must focus on the positives – having your own social life and career while building a relationship with someone you hope you have a future with.

There's a centre for LDRs run by Gregory Guldner, a doctor in California. He's optimistic about LDRs, based on a study he carried out from Purdue University comparing 200 couples in LDRs with 200 who were 'geographically close'. He found that couples in LDRs have the same intimacy and commitment in their relationship as those close by each other. He has some good advice for how to go about an LDR should you choose to do so.

Your biggest fear – and that of most people in LDRs – is that one of you will have an affair. But remember that even people who live together worry about that. Guldner found LDRs had no greater risk of affairs than non-LDRs – it was other factors such as the quality of the relationship and how people feel about infidelity (and if they're likely to take up a chance of opportunistic sex) that determine whether someone strays. You ask if there's any point having an LDR, presumably because you think they can't last, but some research shows that LDRs have no more chance of breaking up than other relationships when factors such as age are accounted for (see 'Homeward Bound', below, as the evidence suggests that moving back together may increase your chances of splitting up). Essentially it's the couple's relationship first, the distance second. You are more likely to have an LDR that works if you assume that if things work out you'll at some stage be geographically close again.

There's not much correlation between how often you see or talk to each other and how likely you are to stay together, unless you go for weeks without speaking and never see each other more frequently than six-monthly intervals. So what you can do to increase your chances? What does matter is setting clear rules: when you will speak and meet again and if you will go on dates with other people. You wouldn't do this if you lived near each other, but some couples feel it is unrealistic to stay monogamous when they live thousands of miles apart. Guldner's research shows that people in LDRs are good at communicating about deep feelings but forget to talk about their humdrum daily lives. Both are essential for intimacy. So tell him when a friend stands you up or a shop assistant is incredibly rude. But don't invest too much emotion in phone calls. Don't be over-sensitive if you hear him yawn or empty the dish washer. Likewise, if one visit doesn't live up to your expectations it doesn't mean the next one won't. All relationships have ups and downs. LDRs need to grow – so have rows and think he's a jerk. If you wear rose-tinted glasses the relationship will die from disillusionment.

A study in the UK by Dr Mary Holmes, from the Department of Sociology at Flinders University in Adelaide, of fourteen academic couples living apart confirmed Guldner's findings of emotional closeness in LDRs and the importance of sharing details of daily life. Holmes concluded that relationships could survive physical distance. Those LDRs that work out usually move closer within four years. And moving closer is really the point of them.

HOMEWARD BOUND

My girlfriend and I have had a long-distance relationship for two years. She found out just before Christmas that she has a new job which means she'll come back to England. We both wanted this to happen, and she'll move in with me. Our relationship has always been romantic but it will be different seeing each other every day. Will we be more or less likely to still be together by the end of next year?

One would hope that it's more likely you'd be together after a year, but it's hard to say. Long-distance relationships (LDRs) are so romantic and difficult that they deserve happily ever after endings. However, although there are self-help books and websites devoted to LDRs, some of the research studies on LDRs changing back to ordinary relationships are not terribly helpful. This is because they've been carried out with either military or undergraduate couples. Military couples have unique problems, as active service distances you from most people, hence their frequent complaint that their partners feel like strangers. So common is this problem that an RAF website directs people to an LDR site called longdistancecouples.com. We'll look at the undergraduate studies (since they're all we've got), but these people are in their early twenties and many people in LDRs are older.

Being geographically close should be good because the research says that it is mundane talking rather than grand gestures that makes relationships strong. So not the red roses at Arrivals but the conversation that goes, 'Now that you're back it's your turn to do the shopping on Fridays.' A paper in the *Journal of Social and Personal Relationships* from Ohio State University found that out of 180 long distance couples who moved closer, 114 stayed together but 66 split up, two thirds of them within the first three months. Most people missed something about their long-distance arrangement: the freedom, novelty value and special sort of closeness they'd felt when living apart. They were four times as likely to notice a new negative quality in their partner as a positive one, usually laziness and immaturity (but then they were students). Jealousy, funnily enough, became more common.

This study found that couples who stayed long distance had the same rate of splitting up as those who moved closer, but another study of undergraduates carried out a year later and published in the same journal found a higher rate in couples who moved closer. It's not clear why there was this difference, but the later study found that LDR couples who were more idealistic about their relationships and had longer gaps between seeing each other were most at risk from splitting up when they moved closer.

Therefore you need to do a rapid and thorough reality check. This can be difficult while you are in an LDR, because there are so many pressures. In an LDR people are more careful to avoid bickering about the trivial, because time together is short and has usually cost money (for example an airfare). In GCRs (geographically close relationships) time is not at such a premium, so you can bicker all day if you want to. In fact, once you become geographically close again it can seem as though quantity has replaced quality. So you will need to readjust to include your partner in your mundane life and to be tolerant of what proximity unearths about each other. Now what could be more romantic than that?

FAITH IN OUR RELATIONSHIP

I am a Muslim woman who is about to tell my traditional parents that I plan to marry my white boyfriend. He will convert, and we won't live together beforehand but even so they may disown me. Will this and our cultural difference make it less likely for us to survive as a couple?

Do cultural differences and parents who'll disown you make you more likely to split up? There isn't a simple yes or no to this question, as you may have expected. Relationship research shows that like marries like and that the support of family and friends helps keep couples together. There isn't much research (and most of it is old) that specifically looks at the risk of divorce among couples of different religious or ethnic groups.

And you are, perhaps surprisingly, still unusual. In England and Wales the latest figures from the Office for National Statistics show that only 2 per cent of marriages are between people of different ethnic groups. Among the Bangladeshi population 3 per cent of people married outside their group, but your boyfriend is actually more unusual than you are. White people are the least likely to marry outside their ethnic group. Even so in some countries inter-ethnic marriages are rising. For example, in America, according to sociologist Michael J. Rosenfeld from Stanford University, inter-ethnic marriages have increased from less than 2 per cent in 1970 to over 7 per cent in 2007.

But whatever the figures, your parents will probably have expected to arrange your marriage. This alone will be shocking for them, although they may have noticed differences between their life and yours. The National Survey of Ethnic Minorities (admittedly in the 1990s) found that most people in south Asian communities had their partners chosen for them by their parents, although even ten years ago people under the age of thirty-four were more likely than older people to want to choose their partner.

The evidence for break-ups is conflicting but is likely to become clearer with more research. As ethnic and religious groups integrate, so they become more likely to marry people from other ethnic and religious groups. Studies of divorce rates have tended to list rather than analyse the reasons. Research from Germany found mixed marriages (except those between German women and Turkish or Yugoslav men) had no higher divorce rates. A study (twenty years old) looking at 10 per cent of divorces in California found shorter marriages between Afro-Caribbean men and white women (by nearly two years). An Australian study in the *Journal of Marriage and Family* found, by re-analysing data from a study of marriages in Hawaii, that mixed marriages did have higher divorce rates but argued that these were due to the beliefs that different ethnic groups have about divorce. If you are from an ethnic group that disapproves of divorce, that will reduce your risk whoever you marry.

There are likely to be other factors at work, but other studies show that where one partner has converted to the other's religion these marriages have lower than average divorce rates (the evidence is strongest among people who convert to the Jewish faith). Conversion is also more likely to encourage family and friends to embrace the relationship.

Without wishing to underestimate the struggle ahead, the fundamentals of long-lasting relationships are romance, companionship, love, support and loyalty. You have to believe these cross cultural boundaries.

TOY BOY OR NOT TOY BOY?

I've always been out with men who were my age or a couple of years older. I split up from someone I'd been living with and it's taken me four years to meet someone I really care about. The problem is he's seven years younger than me. I'm thirty-five. We've talked about getting married. Is this age gap too trivial to worry about?

There's a lot of mythology around age differences in relationships. They are more diverse than you'd think. The Office for National Statistics in England and Wales defines the age gap in marriages as the husband's age minus the wife's age. This reflects the most common pattern and is why you feel a bit uneasy. To some extent you're as old as you behave, but it's hard for couples to share the same values, interests and energy levels if their ages are too disparate. It's going to cause tensions if a woman mid-menopause meets a 25-year-old man who wants his own children (although there are always Italian fertility doctors). Even so, marriage statistics show a surprising range in age differences. Three quarters of marriages are between couples where the woman is between four years older to eight years younger than her man, which leaves a good quarter who have an age gap that's bigger. Your relationship has a –7 age gap, which doesn't seem that off the scale, especially at your ages.

You're actually being quite conformist – in countries as diverse as America and Korea more women are marrying younger men. The proportion of couples in the UK in which the husband was younger than his wife increased from 15 per cent in 1963 to 26 per cent in 2003. Women are more likely to marry younger men if they've been married before. The Office for National Statistics is clear that the age distribution actually reflects indifference (their word) to the age of our partners. An American Association of Retired Persons survey of 3,500 single people aged between forty and sixty found that 34 per cent of women over forty are dating younger men (but it didn't say how much younger). The term 'cougar' is often used to describe older women who date younger men – a reference to the predatory nature of the cat.

There isn't a revolution happening in social norms, but gradually the stereotype of a handful of dysfunctional younger men wanting older woman because it's the nearest they'll get to having sex with their mum and because they can sponge off her larger salary is being eroded. It's becoming more mainstream for perfectly normal men to date older women. As long ago as 1999, a study in the journal *Family Planning Perspectives* discussed data showing that among women up to the age of forty-five (they were looking at pregnancy really, which is why they stopped at forty-five) 29 per cent had a partner who was three to five years older and 7 per cent had one who was six years or more older. A study at California State College found that people believed that relationships with large age gaps of around, for example, eighteen years were less likely to succeed but were very hopeful about what they called 'moderate' gaps of seven years.

Even better, there's research from the University of Oklahoma showing that women married to younger men (by six or more years) live longer than those married to older men. So you'll have more years to enjoy your relationship.

MY VALENTINE

I'm planning to ask my gorgeous girlfriend to marry me on Valentine's Day (we've been together for two years). She complains that I'm not romantic, so I thought I'd surprise her with dinner at a lovely restaurant and a ring. But now I'm getting cold feet that it's not romantic but cheesy. Which is it?

Is it cheesy to ask someone to marry you on Valentine's Day? Surveys show that over 60 per cent of people would find it romantic. If it's not too much of a surprise and your girlfriend wants to marry you she is likely to be thrilled wherever you ask her. What's not to like about someone saying they love you and want to spend the rest of their life with you (unless she's got other plans)?

Rather than worrying about being cheesy, you should worry about being old-fashioned. Don't you know that marriage is on the way out? So you must believe in celebrating commitment, as being married may not make any difference financially. And in this cynical world that makes you seriously romantic.

Proposing is still a key part of the marriage tradition, so give some thought to how you do the asking. A GMTV survey of over 8,500 people found that two thirds of marriages started with a formal proposal – still overwhelmingly by men. Most surveys of attitudes to proposing and Valentine's Day come from companies with a vested interest; jewellers, florists and condom manufacturers (the latter did a survey showing what women most wanted on Valentine's Day was sex). You don't need to get down on one knee: a jeweller's survey of 50,000 Americans found that two thirds of people thought it unnecessary (though younger people in this survey, aged between eighteen to thirty-four, were twice as likely to want to propose on bended knee as older people – presumably because they're still flexible enough to get up afterwards). You don't have to present an engagement ring, as women often like to choose it and like underwear it's embarrassing if it's too tight.

If you want tips on how to be more romantic generally, the surveys all point to personal touch beating the grand gesture. Romance is about small acts of kindness. An American online survey of 250 people found that most preferred a handpicked bunch of wild flowers to twelve long-stemmed out-of-season roses and that women find what's overwhelmingly romantic is their partner doing household chores, cooking them a meal and thoughtfulness such as, 'Are you cold? Why don't you borrow my jacket?' You need also to think about whether you want to propose privately or make a more public gesture. A survey for *Psychology Today* of 250 people found that only just over a third would be put off by a proposal on television or in skywriting or at a public venue. I'm surprised it's not more.

Insurance companies have done their own Valentine's Day surveys. Engagement rings in champagne glasses (glug glug, choke), proposing on top of and then sliding off mountains, and all those candle-lit (oops, my hair's alight) suppers bring many claims. So be aware that romantic gestures have many risks, of which the likelihood of being turned down is probably the least of them.

STOP OR SHOP

My girlfriend and I are buying a house and are about to exchange on the contract. We've been together for two years and now virtually live in my flat, but we've been getting on really badly for the last month. We don't row, we just barely talk to each other. Usually I'm the one to reach out and say sorry, so I expect I'll do it this time. But should we still be moving in together since we're getting on so badly?

Buying a house can put stress on even the strongest relationships, so a month of getting on badly mid-purchase may be reversible. But not if you don't talk to each other. Are you investing in a future together or just buying a property? Did you discuss that future before you applied for a joint mortgage? Thirty years ago living together out of wedlock was frowned upon; until recently it was usually a prelude to marriage. Now it's an end in itself. The figures for how long people who live together, stay together are worse than for those people in marriages but also reflect how casually some couples decide to cohabit (whether or not they buy somewhere together). Cohabitation has become so much the norm that it's hard to know whether most couples think it's any more significant than going on holiday together.

So why do most couples move in together? A study by Dr Sharon Sassler from Ohio State University asked twenty-five people (aged between twenty and thirty-three and living in New York) who had lived together for three months why they'd done so and found that less than a third had ever discussed their future together. Over a half moved in together quite rapidly – within six months. Some said this was because they were so attracted to each other and spent so much time together that it just happened. But these reasons were largely translated into more practical ones around moving in together to save money and for convenience. Do either of these sound familiar?

Data from the British Household Panel Survey show that 70 per cent of first partnerships are cohabitations (and not marriage) and that these last on average two years. They're mostly experimental (as in, just how much will we save on the gas bill?) and never meant to be long-term. Like the New York couples, they often happen because so much time is spent together that migration into one or other's home seems a natural progression. But the two years is only an average; there are cohabiting relationships that last a lifetime. Mostly these started out with that intention. Increasingly, cohabitating relationships will last longer because they will be chosen by more people above marriage.

Before now you may not have needed to brush up on your conflict resolution because you were still in the throes of being easily pleased. But for a future together you can't fall apart over buying a house. Worse things will happen. There's a huge literature on withdrawal behaviour (sulking) in response to conflict, and it basically says: it sucks. Intimacy avoidance, as psychologists call it, is the antithesis of what's needed when the going gets tough. The point of being together (apart from the sex and being able to afford a better property) is to emotionally support each other. So start talking about your future and how you're going to deal with the problems you're bound to have together before exchanging on anything as significant as a house.

HE'S NOT THE ONE

My girlfriend says she loves me but she's not sure if I'm her
soul mate, and because of this she wants to wait before we
move in together. I think she means she's not sure that we
have a future, or am I being over sensitive? Do people really
believe in soul mates?

People really do believe in soul mates, in finding someone
who is 'the one' for them. Soul mates usually means romantic
partners but can, according to various 'soul mate' books,
include friends, siblings or even children, which seems
unlikely. Soul mates can be identified by their ability to talk to
you for hours on first meeting, to understand you better than
your mother does and to be able to finish your sentences for
you. Life with a soul mate is meant to be easy and natural and
lived in a thatched cottage. No wonder so many people want
to know where to find one. The answer should be somewhere
nearby, as soul mates usually share a similar background;
hence their ability to know you so well.

The pursuit of a soul mate is a relatively modern
phenomenon, although Plato is credited with sowing the
seeds, writing in his *Symposium* that humans once had four
legs, four arms and two faces but were cut in half by Zeus,
who feared their power. The halves have been trying to find
each other ever since.

The idea is now so pervasive that a Gallup survey of 1,003
young American adults aged twenty to twenty-nine found that
94 per cent of the single ones (the actual numbers for singles

are not given) believed that 'when you marry you want your spouse to be your soul mate, first and foremost'. Nearly 90 per cent of them also thought 'there is a special person, a soul mate, waiting for you somewhere out there'. Most of them also thought they'd find them. Nearly as many thought the divorce rate was too high. Which begs the question, is there a correlation here?

The problem with the 'only a soul mate will do' philosophy is that it carries a promise of an effortless, perfect relationship. Relationships based on 'we're soul mates' carry a risk of someone bailing out when no one wants to put the bin out or get up for a screaming toddler.

In America Dr Neil Clark Warren set up eharmony.com, an online matching service, out of research he did into marriages. He has defined twenty-nine dimensions for happy marriages and says that to meet a soul mate you have to look beyond the usual five desirable qualities of looks, chemistry, a sense of humour, a good personality and some financial security. Did they have a dysfunctional family (doesn't everyone?), are they as energetic or lazy as you are, do they like being alone, how do they deal with rows? Essentially, Warren's point is that soul mates make for compatible partners, but check thoroughly and go for some objective evidence of compatibility rather than going on some fuzzy feeling that they can read your mind.

Your girlfriend may mean that you're not the one, or that she doesn't know yet. Ask her what she means by a soul mate and how well she thinks you're matched. If she isn't sure, work on getting to know each other better. What you can't do is to pretend to be her soul mate, because you've got your own soul and it's unlikely to go along with it.

GETTING TO 'YES'

My boyfriend has never had relationships lasting longer than a year. He really pursued me but after eight months he's blowing more hot and cold, saying he's busy, that I'm not like he thought I was, and that he's not sure he's ready for a serious relationship. Is there anything I can do to make him feel more committed to me, or am I just not the one for him?

You can only get a commitment phobe to commit if he wants to. And if he wanted to, then he wouldn't be phobic, would he? Commitment phobes look normal (they won't be wearing running shoes for swift retreats) but have a history that gives them away. Watch out for a history of no relationship longer than a year or an accelerated pursuit of you that may be flattering but is actually weird since he can't know much about you. Then you decide (often out of exhaustion) to give it a go and act like a girlfriend, and he swiftly withdraws. He may also become rather critical, usually picking on something you can't change easily such as your family or the shape of your ears.

The commitment phobe can be confused with the total bastard but it's a more clearly defined condition. Women can have it, but it was a phrase invented for men, coined in 1987 by Steven Carter in a book based on interviews with fifty women called *Men Who Can't Love*. Carter nearly called it the Houdini syndrome, after all the men he'd been told about who'd vanished from relationships (one left from a Rome hotel for cigarettes and never returned). Carter defined a behavioural pattern in commitment phobes of pursuit and panic, although he doesn't say why it occurs, preferring to make it clear to women that it's not their fault and that they should get out before their self-esteem disappears along with their partner.

Commitment is usually defined in terms of dedication to your partner and some self-sacrificing element that involves you putting the greater good of the relationship above your own grubby needs. In return, commitment, so the research says, makes you happier, healthier and more resilient to life's occasional thwacks. If you want to know how commitment develops, there's research to tell you. A study of 100 male and 99 female students by researchers at Indiana University Northwest, in the *Journal of Social and Personal Relationships*, asked people what they'd done to change a casual relationship into a serious one. Nearly 40 per cent said they'd seen their partner more and for longer, nearly 30 per cent said they started talking about how they felt about their relationships, and 26 per cent made the relationship more intense by asking for support or personal advice. About 16 per cent asked outright for a more serious relationship. Other studies also show that it's the degree of commitment that men have that decides how positively they view their partner.

If your partner does not exhibit any of the behaviour in the first study then he may not want commitment, and if he doesn't want commitment the other studies suggest he doesn't value you highly and may be sniffing around for alternatives.

I'm guessing here, but 100 per cent of men who don't want to commit, won't do so. They may move in, marry, have kids with you, but these are events and not commitments. For the commitment phobic partner, hyperventilating at the thought of being together for ever, neither you nor anyone else is ever going to be the one, unless they are a trained therapist.

MARRY WITHOUT HASTE

My girlfriend and I have lived together for eight years and have one child. We've decided to get married, but she's read that people who live together first are more likely to divorce than those who haven't. We know couples this has happened to. Should we stay as we are?

There are 2.2 million unmarried couples who live together and have children, an increase of 65 per cent between 1996 and 2006, according to the Office for National Statistics. Living together is a mainstream activity, and over 80 per cent of couples who get married nowadays will have lived together first. The organization One Plus One says that couples live together on average for nearly seven years. About 60 per cent of people in their first living-together relationship get married, which seems rather high when people often start living together for unromantic reasons (such as reducing the cost of living at university).

Much of the research into whether cohabiting first increases your chances of splitting up after you marry was done many years ago when living in sin raised eyebrows and those that did so were more unconventional. This research showed that couples who live together are less happy, more unfaithful, are less confident about their relationships and more abusive to each other than married folk. It also showed that they were twice as likely to divorce as couples who didn't live together first. Men in particular were less committed to cohabiting relationships than married ones.

Why isn't living together a good preparation for marriage? Some researchers speculate that couples carry their lower commitment levels into a casual attitude to marriage. One day they wake up and say, 'We need some new kitchen stuff, let's get married so we can put it on our wedding list.' When the going gets tough this casual approach becomes, 'Let's get divorced.' Simplistic? You'd have to think so.

It may be that couples who embraced living together in the 1970s and 1980s were different from cohabiting couples of today. An Australian study published in *Family Matters* in 2003 found that modern cohabiting couples who married stayed together at similar rates to those who married straight off. Time together was measured from when the couples first got together, whereas in older studies it was measured from the wedding. When they took into consideration other risk factors for divorce, such as youth, poverty, having parents who'd divorced and lower education, the difference fell to 5 per cent after eight years of marriage – still significant, but smaller. Today it would be those who didn't live together first who'd be the odd couples. Yet there may still be a risk of what researchers (from the University of Denver in a paper in *Family Relations*) call a 'slide rather than a decide into marriage' which makes some marriages that started off as cohabiting relationships more vulnerable.

John Ermisch, a statistician at the University of Essex who has studied cohabitation, says that when studies take into account these other risk factors for divorce the risks are eliminated or even reversed. So there is no compelling evidence to stop you getting married. Only the cost and the arguing about the guest list.

LOVE MATCH HAS CATCH

My parents have said I do not have to have an arranged marriage if I don't want to, but I know it will hurt them deeply if I don't. I am unsure what to do. My parents' generation think that arranged marriages are more successful than love matches. What should I do?

Many people still have arranged marriages, especially in Asia, Africa and the Middle East. It's estimated that around 90 per cent of marriages in India are arranged. Now that divorce rates are nudging over one third in some western countries, arranged marriages have attracted some western interest, but they have also had a bad press, being associated with forced marriages and childhood betrothals. Historically, arranged marriages were for the social and economic advancement of families rather than the benefit of individuals. Men were typically older than their wives (and sometimes frankly ancient), and couples were matched for religious belief, caste (where it existed), money, looks (taller men only, please) and the social standing of each family.

Arguments for arranged marriages are based on the perception that young people are impulsive and will choose a partner for superficial reasons such as looks and sexual chemistry. The intense and unrealistic feelings in 'love matches' are bashed by the reality of child-rearing and laundry. This causes many to bail out, or become progressively unhappy. Arranged marriages are more considered, said to 'start cold' and heat up. There are no expectations of happiness, but a duty felt to the families and matchmakers who have brought them together, so working at the relationship is a given. But at the risk of being trivial, you could marry someone you will never find sexually attractive, which is becoming increasingly unacceptable for many young people expected to have arranged marriages. Which may be partly why, as you'll probably know, the arranged marriage market has lightened up. Amit Batabyal, Professor of Economics at the Rochester Institute of Technology, who has researched the economics of arranged marriages, says that modern ones are more flexible. Parents and matchmakers are more like consultants than marriage enforcers, suggesting rather than insisting on a partner.

You'd hope that an arranged marriage would reduce your risk of divorce and make you happier; and Batabyal says divorce rates are higher in countries with mostly love matches. But this may be because economic and political factors prevent divorce in countries where arranged marriages prevail. A report in the *Times of India* says that divorce rates in Mumbai are 40 per cent and in another report that rates are rising in Goa, although the numbers there seem small, at 384 a year. The website divorcerates.org says that India's divorce rate is still around 1 per cent.

So are arranged marriages any happier? A study of 586 married women in Sichuan in China compared those who'd had love matches with those in arranged marriages by asking them how satisfied they were with their relationships. It found women in love matches were happier than those in arranged marriages. Both types of marriage were rated more highly the longer the marriage lasted.

If you are the first generation to try a love match, it will be hard for your parents. You may want to try a half-and-half approach, whereby they suggest people but you don't have to marry them. Agree with them what you will do if you meet someone yourself and what you are looking for. Try to avoid falling for too unusual a choice, as this may be too much for most parents to deal with.

WHAT'S IN A NAME?

My boyfriend and I are getting married. Our relationship is based on love and equality. Our marriage raises the question of sharing a common surname. By giving up my surname I fear I will lose part of my identity and feel subordinated to my boyfriend. Using the same name has practical advantages (more so if we have children), but I cannot help seeing this as an expression of male dominance. My boyfriend likes the idea of one surname but thinks it should be his because it's easier to spell (English) and mine is Dutch. How do other women deal with this problem?

It's down to personal choice. You can keep your maiden name; take his surname and use your maiden name as a middle name; mesh your names to form a new one (for example, Williams marrying Smithson becomes Wilson – why not both lose your identity?) or do a double-barrelled job; take his surname but use your maiden name; or, the most radical option, he could take your name. Confused? Well you can see why most women – around 85 per cent, says a paper in *Population and Societies* called 'The Surname of Married

Women in the European Union' – go the traditional route. There are variations, though: in Italy, for example, women often use both surnames.

Generally, taking the husband's name is a family pleaser (his family is usually the most pleased), some say it's romantic and if you have children you'll be known by their surname anyway. If you choose your husband's surname you will automatically defuse the potentially huge minefield of what surname you put on your children's birth certificate. Some women, however, are opposed to endorsing a patriarchal practice dating from a time when husbands had all the power. If it makes you feel too uncomfortable, don't do it. However, you will still have to cope with people you don't know very well assuming you have adopted your husband's surname.

Traditionally, if you take your husband's surname, you get his whole name. As Mrs John Smith you are completely subordinated – you'll have disappeared. But, thankfully, few use this convention. Some women are more likely to keep their own surname than others. A study in the *Journal of Economic Perspectives* on women's surnames by researchers at Harvard University found that women graduates from Harvard were more likely to keep their surnames if they had higher degrees, jobs in the arts or media and longer careers before marriage. Out of a total of 390 married women in the class of 1980, 44 per cent kept their surname; compared to 32 per cent in 1990 (no actual numbers were given for 1990). The authors speculate that keeping your surname is now less of a feminist issue.

Most women try their partner's name out for size (how does Mrs Emma Roydes sound?). Most research shows women feel either neutral or positive about taking their husband's surname. You may not. Only you can answer the question,

What's in a name? From what you've said it sounds like there's rather a lot.

LOOKING GOOD?

My partner is much better looking than me. I'm not exactly ugly but he's so attractive that people comment on it and I see women drooling over him. He seems oblivious to it, but I wonder if the relationship is doomed because he's so good-looking that people will come on to him all the time. Is our relationship less likely to last?

The stereotype is of a beautiful woman going out with a less attractive man, so you're correct in thinking you're unconventional. Some people would tell you to shut up and stop being so superficial, but not me. This is because the research shows that people choose partners who are similar to them, which includes in the looks department. There's a study called 'Facial Resemblance in Engaged and Married Couples' in the *Journal of Social and Personal Relationships* the hypothesis of which is that couples look like each other because, according to psychological theory, repeated exposure to a stimulus (your face in the mirror) makes that stimulus more attractive. This translates into 'If you look like me, you're gorgeous.' In this study psychology students (who you'd think would have guessed what the study was trying to show) rated the similarity of male to female faces in sixty paired photographs. About half of the pairs were either engaged or married, the others were randomly put together (although how wasn't said). The real couples were rated as more similar in standard measures of attractiveness, such as how symmetrical their face was and how prominent their cheek bones were (think Balkan supermodel).

If you have defied the laws of nature and are with a person much better looking than you, what will happen? Reducing your relationship to a mercenary transaction, you may have other things that make you attractive to him: conversation, affection, stability or money. If your relationship is just about looks, the research doesn't bode well. A 1980s study from the University of Maryland compared attractiveness levels in 123 couples (on a nine-point scale) and gave them a 35-page relationship questionnaire. They found that couples in the most serious relationships were more likely to be of similar attractiveness. Nine months later, those who were less similar were more likely to have split up. Men who were more attractive (regardless of how good-looking their partner was) were more likely to admit to thinking about other relationships (except those who were married).

Most of the research has looked at levels of attractiveness early on in relationships. A study from the University of California in Los Angeles delved deeper into the influence that levels of attractiveness have in more-established relationships. James McNulty and his colleagues analysed how eighty-three couples, on average together for forty-five months, discussed a personal problem, while researchers ranked the facial attractiveness of each person. The research team found that the more attractive husbands were less supportive of their wives, especially when their wives were less attractive than they were. This, they concluded was because good-looking men have their pick of women and may be less ready to be satisfied and supportive in their own relationships. As they admit, however, this is speculation; the study shows an association, not proof that good-looking men are bastards.

It's also worth knowing that other studies show we overestimate how attractive our partners really are (and how likely our relationships are to last for ever) – such are the positive illusions that love brings. That said, his looks seem to be an issue for you and you'll need to deal with it. He's chosen to be with you, so instead of insisting you don't believe him, enjoy his looks and see if his personality is just as attractive.

Jealousy and Affairs

MEN IN UNIFORM

My partner and I have been together for six years, and after three he joined the police. Friends of ours are full of stories of affairs. I trust my partner and we're planning our wedding, but is there evidence that working in a tight-knit group over unsocial hours induces affairs?

It's hard to know how reliable the statistics are on how many people have affairs at work. A survey of 1,072 workers from different industries by the company Human and Legal Resources found 61 per cent had had affairs at work and one third of these people were already married. Most affairs occurred in the leisure and tourism industry and the least in healthcare. This doesn't tell us much, because both types of jobs can involve long hours, but arguably it's more stressful being a doctor than a holiday rep. There's good evidence that unsocial hours causes unhappiness in relationships – a study of 1,668 married couples by the University of Nebraska-Lincoln found the risk of divorce increased from 7 per cent to 11 per cent over the three years of the study (which was statistically significant). Other surveys suggest that if you work long hours, surrounded by members of the opposite sex, you may be susceptible to an affair. But it depends on the person's views on infidelity and their existing relationship.

There are no national statistics linking occupation and divorce, because they aren't routinely collected by statistics offices. There are no employment questions on divorce papers. There is some rampant mythology around police marriages – one US website quotes a 75 per cent divorce rate, and another a rate seven times higher than average, comparable, it says, to doctors' divorce rates. But there is good evidence that rates are not higher than average among doctors, so the statistics on police divorces may not be reliable either. A study in the *New England Journal of Medicine* of 1,118 married doctors found that just some specialities such as psychiatry had only slightly higher rates. Both doctors and policemen look after the public, but in a direct comparison of attractiveness police officers may win because of the uniform and handcuffs.

Researchers from the University of California, Berkeley looked at the effects of stress at work on nineteen male police officers and their wives, asking them to keep thirty day stress diaries and watching them interact in a laboratory. The researchers were looking for the early warning signs of an imploding relationship – the inability of a couple to regulate their emotions and remain civil to each other. They found that although the police officers were stressed, their wives tried very hard to be civil to them. Couples did cope because their partners supported them. The researchers were clear, however, that continued job stress is toxic for relationships.

Dr Ellen Kirschman, an American psychologist who is an expert on police officers and relationships, says they do

not have more affairs or divorces than anyone else. They
are psychologically screened and so should start off at least
above average for mental health. You can forget about affairs.
She says that police officers are more likely to damage their
relationships by being distant emotionally and anxious about
the vulnerability of their family (bringing their work home
with them). It's this that can be hard to live with.

NEW COMPANY

*My girlfriend has a new job in a big company that is known
for socializing after work. We've been together (happily) for
three years, but now she'll meet new men and go out drinking
more at this job than at her old one. Am I being insecure in
worrying that I'll lose her?*

Opportunity is a risk factor for infidelity but not the foregone
conclusion you think it is. The many studies on infidelity
show that it depends on three main factors. They sound rather
premeditated, and it's certain that your girlfriend won't be
using them as a conscious checklist. Firstly it depends on
how likely she is to think she can find someone better than
you, secondly how much she has invested and thus can lose
in your relationship, and finally her beliefs on infidelity. Most
people (UK surveys show around 80 per cent) disapprove
of infidelity, especially in long-standing relationships. But
around a quarter of people will be unfaithful and rationalize

it in various ways – being unfulfilled (i.e. not having enough sex), being underwhelmed by their partner, overwhelmed by someone else or under the influence. For many people it really is an inconsequential act – it only ceases to be if you, the partner, find out about it.

The UK's Sexual Attitudes and Lifestyles Survey found that women who work are three times more likely to be unfaithful to a partner as one who stays at home (where they only meet postmen and plumbers). Other studies show an increase among people who travel overnight for work (hotels have sex appeal), those who are less happy in their relationship and those who have been unfaithful before. Studies from America show that the availability of eligible partners does increase the likelihood of infidelity, especially where women work in areas where they are outnumbered by men. Some American companies have tried to ban relationships at work and made it clear that if people get together at work they must tell their bosses and one of them should find another job. Clearly, affairs at work do happen, and a survey by the UK company Human and Legal Resources of 1,072 workers found that 61 per cent had had an office romance, and in a third of these one or both partners were married. There is evidence from other studies that the likelihood of an affair depends on the availability of partners, A Swedish study found that the divorce rate was 70 per cent higher for a person working in a place where they were the only person of their sex. The sex ratios at work are likely to be more influential on rates of couples splitting up than forming in the first place.

But this doesn't mean your girlfriend has any desire to stray. If she's committed to you, she won't send out or receive incoming messages of availability. Psychologists do have suggestions to affair-proof relationships which sound nauseating but work better than the only other

alternative – of sabotaging your partner's career. You have
to have a conversation for at least 40 minutes every day, go
on dates four times a week, make cups of tea for her and
be affectionate. You could suggest meeting her after work
sometimes, but stop being insecure because it will look
desperate. The odds are against her going off with someone
else so your insecurity, happily, is likely to be redundant.

IS SHE FAITHFUL?

*I think my girlfriend is having an affair. She's been working
closely with a man who I've never liked, because he's known
to be lecherous, and she's been coming home very late some
nights. She's definitely more distant. Shall I ask her outright
or snoop around?*

The choice is yours. There's a whole industry feeding the need
people have to know if their partner is cheating. Some people
may worry with good reason; others will be vulnerable because
they're insecure. If you want proof you can try anything from
online kits to private detectives and sophisticated surveillance
techniques that tell you every move your partner makes on
her computer and the calls she's deleted from her mobile
phone. You may want to go for CheckMate, a kit that can
detect traces of semen that linger for many hours after sex.
The company suggests you test creatively: don't just go for
underwear, try towels and socks. Love Detector is a 'simple,

friendly service' that analyses how your partner feels about you by using voice-analysis technology. You call the love detector number and then your love rat of a partner and when the chat is over the company provides an in-depth analysis on how embarrassed she was. What it won't tell you is if she's having sex with that guy you're worried about.

The more traditional rifling through her things (for example credit-card statements, diary), watching for suspicious computer or mobile phone behaviour and sniffing for the smell of someone else's aftershave is cheaper. Even more cost effective is the approach quoted by Menstuff.com, which says that instinct accurately detects infidelity for 85 per cent of men and 50 per cent of women. The figure is unsubstantiated, but that gut-wrenching feeling you get when the person you're with is somehow different is very real. Infidelity can make people intensely angry as well as sad.

It's also quite common. In the *Handbook of Divorce and Romantic Relationship Dissolution*, researchers Julie H. Hall and Frank D. Fincham quote over two thirds of college students as being unfaithful; studies usually come up with figures for married couples that range from a quarter to up to 60 per cent of men and 40 per cent of women (there is a wide variation in the surveys and studies, as how they are done determines how honest people are). Researchers used to think men had affairs for the sex and women for the love they were missing at home. Now that we all know women enjoy sex too, they think it's mostly just about more sex for both men and women. Many affairs do start at work. The research organization One Plus One says that women are three times as likely to have an affair if they work away from home, even if they travel infrequently. An Australian study of 119 people (aged between seventeen and twenty-five) found that affairs among couples who were dating were more likely to happen when there were attractive people around to be unfaithful with and when the relationship was not very happy. Both of which are sufficiently shallow reasons to be a worry.

You may get proof and decide to challenge your girlfriend, or you may let events unfold. An MSNBC survey of 70,288 readers found that affairs mostly finished in six months. If you ask her she may lie or, worse, accuse you of paranoia. The MSNBC survey found about half of both sexes had cheated but only 6 per cent admitted it on direct questioning (although the numbers asked is not given). You may want to improve your relationship anyway. Tell your girlfriend how much she means to you (if it's not much then her infidelity's less of a blow), go out together, call her at work to say hi (not as in, 'Hi, are you sitting on X's lap?'), be interested in what she is doing (but don't scare her). If you do find out she is having an affair that's actually the easy bit. It's far harder to make your relationship work afterwards.

ME OR THE MISSUS?

I'm in love with a man who is married with two children. I met him through work and we became friends, but for two years we've been lovers. He hasn't been close to his wife for years and says he won't stay in an unhappy marriage once the children are older. But, realistically (and selfishly), is there any chance he'll leave her for me?

Will your lover and father of two leave his wife for you? You'd be hard pushed to find anyone who'd encourage you to hang around to find out. Not because it's morally wrong to have an affair with a married father of two (not ideal behaviour though, is it?) but because the odds are not in your favour. There aren't many numbers, but those that exist make grim reading.

I could only find studies published in books, not in peer-reviewed psychology journals. Firstly there's a much quoted study by Dr Jan Halper, an American psychologist, in her book *Quiet Desperation – The Truth about Successful Men*. Halper interviewed 4,126 'successful' male business leaders and executives. She found that 88 per cent of them were equally successful in the bedroom as the boardroom, having had at least one affair. But she found that only 3 per cent of those men left their wife for the woman they were having an affair with. Dr Lana Staheli, in her book *Affair-Proof Your Marriage*, claims that less than 10 per cent of people divorce their spouses to marry their lovers and when they do up to 70 per cent of these marriages also end in divorce. An even more pessimistic failure rate of 75 per cent is quoted by psychiatrist Frank Pittman in his book *Private Lies: Infidelity and the Betrayal of Intimacy* which is based on interviews with 100 adulterous couples (his term, not mine). Pittman says these marriages don't work out either because reality bites (everyday living together is not as glamorous as snatched hotel sex), there's too much guilt or the person who initiated the affair is not trusted not to do so again. As the saying goes, when a man marries his mistress, he creates a job vacancy.

This is not to say your man is leading you on – only that he may be. Ruth Houston, an infidelity expert who set up infidelityadvice.com, has interviewed around 10,000 cheaters and cheatees (as she calls them) over thirteen years. She says that most men who have affairs aren't unhappy in their relationships – they mostly do it for the sex or to boost their egos. She agrees with other researchers that they don't want to leave their wives. Her own research (which started when she discovered her husband, now her ex, was having an affair) finds that if their wives find out and they do leave they usually want to start afresh. Completely afresh.

Of course, you may have a different experience. The problem in asking, 'Will he leave her for me?' is that it's the wrong question. 'Should I get out and start seeing someone else?' is a better one, with the more optimistic answer – yes.

TOO MANY COOKS

After several failed monogamous relationships my partner believes that, for him, open polyamory is a more honest and natural way to accommodate loving more than one person. Is there any evidence that such relationships can work satisfactorily and might they even be better than secretive relationships, which are common and cause vast numbers of broken monogamous relationships?

Polyamory is having more than one relationship at the same time with the knowledge and consent of all partners involved. There is meant to be 'love' involved, which distinguishes it from swinging – polys, as they are known, are meant to have sex within another loving relationship and not just throw their car keys into a bowl in some stranger's living room. Polys argue that monogamy is dishonest because lots of people are unfaithful and that it's unnatural (no wonder, they argue, that infidelity is rife). What little research there is shows that for polyamory to work, you both have to want it. But there's more. Couples have to be able to communicate well, respect each other and agree that their relationship is the 'primary' one, which should be preserved. You also need to be a stranger to jealousy or possessiveness (both much more common than infidelity). If your relationship is this strong you would think it could survive monogamy.

Some polys live in communities and share the fridge and childcare, but most don't. Since they don't all wear badges saying 'I'm a poly' it is hard to identify them and undertake research on their lifestyle. Estimates of how common polyamory is are likely to be wildly inaccurate – there are no meaningful ones in the UK, while in America enthusiasts estimate there are half a million, but acknowledge that many of them won't know what polyamory is and will think they are just having sex with other people sometimes. Polyamory is more common among male couples, with estimates by polyamorists (but no one else) of one third being polys.

There isn't good evidence to suggest that polys are any happier than monogamous couples. A study in the *Journal of Family and Economic Issues* of 150 Dutch couples in open marriages that were not defined as polyamorous but seemed to have similar rules, showed only that they were as happy and well adjusted as monogamous couples, not that they were more so. Since no one need sneak off to have an affair, are these relationships more enduring than monogamous ones?

Poly supporters often cite a study by Elaine Cook in the *Electronic Journal of Human Sexuality* that, they claim, shows that poly relationships last at least as long as monogamous ones. But the study is only of seven couples who had been together for five years, and Cook is a poly who was friends with four of the couples. Her conclusions, that polyamory works because despite other choices people stay in their primary relationship out of love and a 'connection', are therefore not reliable. Sorry. There are other studies: one in the *Family Coordinator* in 1975 of 380 people who had been in open relationships for ten years showed that they were happy and that their relationship with their partner had improved. But there was no comparison group and no studies of people who drop out of polyamory.

There are lots of poly fans, but most people still go with monogamy. A study of over 33,500 people in twenty-four countries published in the *Journal of Sex Research* found that 85 per cent disapproved of extramarital sex. If you can deal with social disapproval on a global scale that's great. Just make sure you don't become a poly to keep your partner, as there's no evidence it will do that.

GREEN-EYED MONSTER

I have a lovely boyfriend who I think is gorgeous, but when he talks to other women at parties I feel jealous, and when he goes out after work I get all tortured imagining him flirting with other women. I've got no reason to think he would be unfaithful, and he always reassures me. My jealousy is irritating him now – how can I stop it?

Jealousy is so painful and widespread that you'd have to suspect it exists for a reason. Poets, such as Keats, have often suffered terribly from it (he always suspected his beloved Fanny Brawne was out partying with men while he was lying on his sick bed, though she wasn't), so it may serve a creative purpose. Evolutionary psychologists say that jealousy is an evolved behaviour that kicks in when there's a threat to reproductive resources (that'll be your boyfriend). Making sure that no one else is after your boyfriend ('mate guarding' as its called) may be especially strong for women around ovulation. The threat may be real or imagined, although it's unclear why mate guarding has to make you feel sick to the pit of your stomach or want to mutilate your partner's clothes. But then evolution is an imperfect process.

Women are traditionally threatened by attractive rivals, men by rivals who earn more than they do. At the heart of jealousy is the fear that you've lost control over someone else's feelings – that they've gone off and had feelings for, or just a good time with, someone else. But studies do find that some people are unhealthily jealous of their partner's hobbies or families, anything that takes time from them.

Much of the research asks people how jealous they would feel about hypothetical events, so it is not that reliable. A questionnaire survey of 132 people by the University of Wisconsin-Madison looked at the connection between uncertainty in relationships and jealousy. It found that people in less certain relationships were most jealous about anyone they thought their partner might want to have sex with. More secure couples felt most jealous about their partner becoming emotionally close to someone else. They found that personal insecurity didn't make people more jealous – so it's not some self-worth problem you need to deal with.

You should ask yourself what you're worried about. Is it that someone else is enjoying his company – or that someone will see this? Or is it that you'll lose him? Other studies show jealousy can be corrosive to relationships. If you major on interrogation, you'll drive yourself bonkers and him as far away as possible. You need to remember not only that he's with you and no one else but that he seems to want to avoid making you jealous. How committed is that?

Do your best to minimize your jealousy, but be aware that in small amounts it can spice up a relationship. A study of 226 people in the journal *Communication Reports* found that jealousy wasn't always negative – couples could laugh about it and find it a positive thing that their partner thought them desirable by other people. Being shallow folk, a jealous episode can make sex more passionate. Try to deal with it using humour and honesty rather than distancing yourself or getting cross. It doesn't sound like there's cause for jealousy and you seem well motivated to stop it. For now at least you sound more irritated by your jealous feelings than he is.

FLIRT ALERT

My boyfriend is always flirting with other women. He has a reputation for being a flirt, and I always hope there won't be an attractive woman when we go out because he'll talk to her and ignore me. He also gets flirty texts. Should I just accept that's who he is and not get jealous, or can I make him stop?

Flirting, says a report from the Social Issues Research Study in Oxford, 'is the foundation of civilization'. Okay, so the report was funded by Martini and there were no references, but you can see that flirting could be essential to the survival of the human species. But what's wrong with your boyfriend flirting only with you?

To accuse someone of flirting, you must think there is some sexual intent. Otherwise they would just be good at talking to women (or men). There are moves in flirting that overlap with those of good conversationalists: listening intently, making eye contact and touching to make a point (an arm, not a thigh). Other techniques such as eyebrow flashing (as in 'I really know you, don't I?'), saying 'You look gorgeous in that,' leaning towards someone and looking at their cleavage (it happens) are 100 per cent flirtatious. Flirtatious speech is more animated; flirts like to laugh and to look at the mouth of whoever they're flirting with. Flirting can be, and often is, harmless and enjoyable and is arguably an essential life skill.

That said, although a survey by *Men's Health* of 1,500 men found that 94 per cent of men did not consider flirting to be unfaithful, this doesn't excuse men from doing it when their girlfriend is at the bar. Over two thirds of men said they would be flattered rather than jealous if a gorgeous man flirted with their girlfriend. Oh, really?

But there are some fine lines. The same proportion said that suggestive comments and flirty emails were fine, but kissing, unsurprisingly, was not. An international study in the *Journal of Sex Research* of 877 male and 1,194 female students from countries including Ireland and the Netherlands found that hugging or dancing with someone else did not make partners jealous, whereas flirting did. Even when partners discussed sexual fantasies it did not create the jealousy that flirting did.

And it may bother women more than men. A study in *Personal Relationships* of 219 college students showed that more women than men considered flirting to be unfaithful. This does not mean they don't do it themselves.

Flirting, as you've found, is also done via mobiles (although only 8 per cent of people flirt this way, according to a survey of over 5,000 people in the UK by YouGov) and through social networking sites such as Facebook. The distance and unreality of the medium can make messages become rapidly more explicit.

Even if your boyfriend is an innocent flirt he could tone it down a bit. You could ask him why he flirts. Is he insecure (use another term of course), does he want a response from you, does he even know how horrible it makes you feel? He probably doesn't take the flirting further, but that doesn't mean you should accept it. If you can't make him stop flirting, then at least watch how he does it and pick up some useful tips for finding your next boyfriend.

TRUTH OR DARE?

I had a short affair with a woman I used to work with (we did a stressful project together). I really regret it, but I don't know whether to tell my wife about my affair or not. Is there a 'good' way to tell her?

It's a case of being damned if you do tell and damned if you don't. On balance you may do more damage to your relationship by not telling her, but the evidence for this is too flimsy to be reliable. Infidelity is unpopular with everyone; surveys show that over 80 per cent of people think it's wrong, largely for moral reasons. Yet people still do it. The Sexual Attitudes and Lifestyles Survey in the UK found that 14.6 per cent of men and 9 per cent of women had been unfaithful in the past year. Rates are higher in casual relationships.

Most people in committed relationships have another (even half-hearted) go at staying together after an affair. How someone finds out about the affair does seem to make a difference, but it's not clear how much this influences the eventual outcome. A study of 105 college students (men and women) in the *Journal of Social and Personal Relationships* shows that when the person admitted (unasked) to an affair, 56 per cent of couples stayed together, compared to 14 per cent when the partner found out on direct questioning. Having to ask and then being told confers a double whammy – your partner not only cheated but lied. Relationships do recover from infidelity, and being married improves your chances of survival. Being miserably married for years, or having an affair to get back at your partner, however, do not.

There's no 'good' way to tell your wife, only a less bad way. This is a grim business. Your wife will be angry, but worse for your relationship she will torture herself by running through the gory details in her mind and wondering what's wrong with her that you had to have sex with someone else. She will believe she can no longer trust you.

There are no data on what will happen if you don't tell her or on the chances of her finding out anyway. But studies on secrets in relationships show it requires a huge effort not to blurt them out, and concentrating in order to keep your mouth shut can create distance between you. But then divorce creates distance too.

Telling her yourself gives you some control over how she finds out. You can give a consistent story, making sure you sound incredibly sorry and explain why you cheated – cite circumstances rather than blaming your wife. Promise both to never do it again and to do your best to make it right. Once the horror has faded you can have an honest go at repairing and improving your relationship, but don't expect instant forgiveness. That lightness of spirit you may have after telling her about your affair will be at her expense. She'll be the one who's now burdened with it.

Complete honesty is not the best policy, though, so stick to essential facts. Don't ever be drawn into details such as what the other woman looked like or what sex toys you used, the luxury hotels you used them in – obvious stuff, perhaps. Even worse would be a frank discussion on how much you felt for whoever you had the affair with (unless it was very little). There's only so much disclosure a relationship can take, however well it's done.

JUST GOOD FRIENDS

My boyfriend has a close female friend from his last job who he sees without me. I don't really like it, and my friends think I'm stupid to let him see her. Most men I've been out with started out as 'friends'. Should I trust him, or is it naive to think he's only friends with her?

The 'Can men and women just be friends?' question is rather complicated. Surveys show that many romantic relationships start off as friendships (over half), but this may be because one person is attracted to the other and chooses a let's-be-mates rather than a direct approach. A poll on the women's website handbag.com found overwhelming support (83 per cent of the 1,811 votes cast) for the idea of men and women being able to be platonic friends. But, oops, nearly half of women said some male friends were ex-lovers and one third of women secretly lusted after their male friends but didn't act on it because of the risk to their friendship. Men are more likely to be attracted to their women friends than vice versa – a survey by MarketTiers of 1,000 people in the US found that one third of men fancy one of their close female friends.

Some psychologists believe cross-sex relationships really can be platonic because of the phenomenon of friendship attraction. Characteristics that people value in friends they also want in lovers – but there's more of an emphasis on lust and physical attraction in romantic relationships. In platonic friendships any physical attraction has to be ignored or at least not acted upon. Friendships that work are highly valued, with men saying they enjoy talking to someone about things other than sport and women feeling they get to understand men a bit more.

Yet these relationships are potentially more complicated than same-sex friendships. Vickie Harvey, a researcher from California State University, was driven to study them because of her intense friendships with some male work colleagues. She asked 120 college students to keep a journal for sixteen weeks, each discussing one platonic friendship. She found that while some friendships start out as testing grounds for relationships, that moment usually passes. However, at some stage a quarter of them had kissed or held hands, although generally the relationship quickly shifted back to being platonic. Most of the students wanted to keep their friendship platonic even if they felt attracted to each other.

So your boyfriend probably is just friends with her and you can trust him because he's chosen to go out with you. Some men are more able than others to be friends with women, and you'll have a good idea of whether your boyfriend is one of them – especially if you invite yourself along one evening. He would be smart to introduce you to her (and if he doesn't you should push for it), since if you get to know her you're likely to be less concerned about their relationship. In the meantime watch out for warning phrases of growing intimacy, such as, 'I told X all about our fight in the car/sex in the garden.' No one likes a cross-sex friend knowing personal stuff about their relationship. You may want to take some preventative measures to protect your relationship, like asking him specific questions about his work and interests and how he feels about things – both trivial and profound. Make sure you have time together and go out and have fun. Basically be a mate to him yourself.

Break-ups or Make-ups?

REVENGE IS SOUR

My boyfriend has always flirted in front of me and made it clear he's interested in other women, and now he's dumped me for someone he works with. I'm so angry that all I can think of is how to get back at him and hurt him. Would taking some revenge make me feel better, and if so what should I do?

You're clear on why you want revenge (and well-defined goals are good) but any idea that you'll feel better afterwards may be misguided. However, it's worth reviewing the common methods of revenge for women, which include phoning sex lines and leaving the phone off the hook, burning clothes (his), telling work colleagues and friends he's a coke fiend (assuming he isn't) and having sex with his best friend. Posting intimate videos online is usually a man thing.

In a study of eighty-eight Canadians by researchers at the University of Calgary, the most popular methods of revenge were flirting with friends or enemies of their ex, keying their car, breaking something they loved (not their arms or legs), writing nasty notes to their ex, and gossiping (with a megaphone) about how useless their ex was in bed. The most popular revenge method for people still with the partner they're angry with was either flirting in front of them or the silent treatment (not much use if you're no longer together).

So pick your revenge weapon of choice by all means, but will it make you feel better? In trying to get even you probably want your ex to feel hurt and humiliated. Ideally even more than you are. A study by Stephen Yoshimura at the University of Montana asked 152 people (average age twenty) what acts of revenge they had carried out, what they had wanted to achieve by them and how they felt afterwards. They found that most people who'd spread rumours about their ex, taken their stuff or damaged their property felt anxious and sorry rather than joyful afterwards. But most of all they still felt angry. People wanted their revenge to punish their ex and to make themselves feel more in control. But taking revenge only seemed to make them feel marginally better and rather more thoroughly miserable. It's hard to do things you'd normally think are wrong – even when you're doing them to a complete bastard. Revenge, unfortunately, is for most people not a jolly act of retribution.

So why not try the traditional ways of making yourself feel sexy, and therefore making your ex regret his actions – starving yourself to a size zero or buying some breast implants. I'm not being serious. However angry you are now, the odds are you'll be just as angry if you take revenge. Just as you'd be more hurt if you were still with him than without him. It sounds like you're well rid of him. You'll feel much better if you send him a thankyou card instead.

POST TRAUMATIC LOVE DISORDER

Is there such a thing as post traumatic love syndrome? If there isn't, there should be. I split up from my girlfriend three years ago after a stormy relationship and haven't seen her since, but I can't stop thinking about her and missing her badly every day. What is wrong with me?

The break-up of a relationship can be one of life's most traumatic events. Many studies document the depression and heart disease (it would be heart disease) that occur in some people after divorce. However, it's not only divorce that can wreak havoc on one's physical and emotional wellbeing. A Canadian study of 5,254 women and 4,521 men aged between twenty and sixty-four, in the *Journal of Marriage and Family*, found the same effects for people who split up after living together (a rise in depression and decline in physical health, in this study felt more by men). The break-up of any strongly felt relationship can be intensely traumatic.

There probably should be such a thing as post traumatic love syndrome. It would have to be considered as a lesser condition than post traumatic stress disorder (PTSD), because it doesn't involve a life-threatening incident such as an act of terrorism (being a hostage of love doesn't count) or plane crash, but it may share symptoms. These include reliving the moment, avoidance and emotional numbing (you avoid places and people who remind you of what happened) and being hypervigilant in case it happens again.

In less psychiatric and more everyday terms you'll be less open, more irritable and anxious. You may feel distant from other people and less interested in just about everything. Being traumatized after any event is linked to feeling helpless about what happened during the event itself – so you may feel you couldn't change things even if you wanted to. Did you initiate the split? A study from the University of Colorado of 144 newly separated husbands and wives found that people who didn't initiate the split were likely to suffer more afterwards, feeling out of control and more distressed. It didn't seem to matter how unhappy their relationships were beforehand – they suffered just the same. You feel that you had little or no control over the relationship break-up, but your ex girlfriend probably felt the same way.

Just as people with PTSD are more likely to get depressed and develop drug and alcohol problems, so are divorced men. Has this happened to you? Three years to get over your girlfriend is not pathological, but it isn't healthy. Getting over this event requires reorganization – of your thoughts and your life. You should talk it through with someone you can trust. If this doesn't help, you need to train yourself to think about it differently. Most importantly, you need to be less preoccupied by thoughts of your ex. Over 75 per cent of people with PTSD recover with time, and now that you've had time you should consider some treatments. Ones that may work for a traumatized lover include relaxation therapy, cognitive therapy (which through talking to a therapist gets you to look at things differently) and eye-movement treatments that desensitize you to the trauma. Traditional psychotherapy is a larger investment that could take another three years. Many people do think about their ex's every day. You'll know you're over her when you think about her and it doesn't hurt.

TEARS BEFORE BEDTIME

For the last three years I've gone out with friends to some great New Year's Eve parties. Then around midnight I'm suddenly overwhelmed by thinking about my ex-boyfriend who I split up with three years ago. I lived with him for nearly four years, and although I feel I'm over him, at this time each year it's like it happened yesterday. It's so embarrassing – usually I start crying really loudly in the kitchen. Why does it still hit me so hard and will it ever get better?

Why, I wonder, do you cry really loudly instead of stuffing tissues into your mouth to keep the noise down? After three years of audible sobbing you must have very good friends to still get invited out.

Alcohol, the countdown to New Year and 'Auld Lang Syne' are failproof catalysts for nostalgic longing. New Year's Eve can be a good excuse for crying about any loss; a mourning of the old as much as a celebration of the new. And if thoughts about your ex are to pop up at any time, it's at 'Happy New Year!' time when you start thinking, 'So how happy am I?', 'Wasn't I happier with X?' and 'What's X doing right now?'

I'm not unsympathetic. There is some often quoted research, the original paper of which I have never been able to find, that quotes an average of one month per year of a relationship to get over someone. Other research into marriages that break up suggests it takes a year and half for people to start feeling happy again. If you aren't with anyone yet, the odds are that

you soon will be. But nothing can really insure you against
memories on New Year's Eve. Should you block out upsetting
thoughts about ex-lovers? The research is inconclusive.
The studies are fairly primitive – one from the University
of Virginia measured electrical impulses across the skin of
seventy young people, and found that suppressing thoughts of
ex-lovers (when the person was still sad about them) increased
stress and anxiety levels. Some neuroscientists from the
University of South Carolina got excited when they found that
measuring brain activity in eleven women who were mourning
the loss of recent relationships pinpointed the exact parts of
the brain that felt grief. So brain surgery could help. Only
kidding.

Many studies show that you are more likely to get over
someone if you initiated the split, have a career to keep
you busy, have a large social network of friends to tell you
that you can do better and, to a lesser extent, have a new
lover. New relationships generally do help, though on New
Year's Eve there's the risk that a few drinks and a dollop of
selective memories can make any current partner seem less
desirable than a former flame. Psychologists have published
reams on the attachment theory of relationships, saying that
relationships create a strong biological bond that causes
physical and emotional distress at separation. Some people,
perhaps you, are predisposed to react more strongly to the loss
of a relationship. This may be because you got so attached that
you're still struggling to let go. He is not your mum or dad so
it's okay to forget about him.

Please don't cry this year. If he pops into your head shove him
back out again or concentrate on his bad points. Otherwise
your sobbing will upset people who don't know you and,
worse, when the clock chimes twelve, no one will want to give
you a new year's kiss.

UNFAIR AFFAIR

I had a brief relationship with a woman who was the friend of a work colleague. She ended it because it 'wasn't going anywhere'. I was devastated because I felt I was falling in love with her, and now I can't stop thinking about her. It's been a month now and sometimes I drive past her house on purpose and feel like a stalker. How could I have got it so wrong and how can I get over her?

Unrequited love is nearly a universal experience. It is the stuff of literature – Cyrano de Bergerac had it badly but carried it nobly, and Jane Austen's heroines were highly susceptible – but things usually came good in the end. In real life, where unrequited love usually stays that way, it causes deep despair. A study of 155 men and women by researchers at Cape Western Reserve University in Ohio, published in the *Journal of Personality and Psychology*, found that only 2 per cent of them had never experienced unrequited love (defined as an intense, passionate yearning that is not reciprocated). The study counted being both rejected by and rejecting someone as an 'experience'. Men were a third more likely than women to have suffered unrequited love. Those who did the rejecting felt guilty (claiming overall to feel worse than those they rejected) but also irritated by any attempts to win them back.

Some people are more prone to unrequited love than others, so you want to be careful, even in the midst of your grief, not to make it a habit. It may sound obvious, but if you are anxious about relationships, emotionally needy, and fall in love at the drop of a hat, then the main thing you're courting is disappointment. Passion is great, but too much, too soon, can push people away; a little restraint is not just attractive, it's essential for self-preservation. A study in the *Journal of Social and Personal Relationships* of over 300 men and women's experiences of falling in love found that this blissful state was triggered not only by the desirability of the other person but also by a confidence that the loving feeling was mutual. Most people fall in love with someone they are pretty sure loves them. It just works better that way. It is possible to misread someone else's signals, and other studies show that rejected lovers often feel they were 'led on'. But if you keep getting it wrong then it's you and not them who you need to talk to.

It's also possible for long-term relationships to end with one partner still in love with the other. This is more painful, and often the announcement comes out of the blue. But in a short-lived relationship you should be able to move on relatively painlessly. Loving and losing is romantic, but stalking is obsessive. Stop now. Grieve for another week maximum, get out there, keep busy, try again, and tell yourself it happens to everyone. No one wants to dent your enthusiasm for love, but it's an activity in which receiving is as important as giving.

CUDDLING DEFICIENCY

I have been with my man for almost four years and we love each other deeply. Unfortunately, he struggles with demonstrating his feelings. His lack of affection makes me feel lonely and unattractive. He says he doesn't need affection, although he cuddles me during sleep. He is unable to relax

during love making and behaves like an embarrassed
teenager in bed. How can I make him see that I am a
woman and need a smattering of affection and the odd
compliment?

Your man is not comfortable with intimacy and it gets worse
the more intimate you get. But he sounds like a nice guy;
perhaps the cuddling in bed redeems him. You also seem
confident that he loves you, and that confidence must derive
from something he says or does. He must behave as though
he loves you. His problems with demonstrating his feelings,
at least physically, are nothing personal so it's a shame you're
feeling lonely and unattractive.

Might you feel better if you knew that women are generally
more touchy in relationships than men? The evidence,
however, isn't clear. A study in the *Journal of Social and
Personal Relationships* had researchers selecting 154 couples
from cinema queues and observing how often they touched
within a two-minute period. They then went up to the couples
and asked them how long they'd been together. They found
there were no differences between how often men and women
started touching their partner, and, as you might expect,
longer-term couples were less likely to touch each other. But
this didn't mean they weren't close. The longer-term couples
rated themselves closer than other couples – they just didn't
show as much affection to each other. At least not when
queuing. The researchers didn't follow them home.

Intimacy is important in relationships because when
reciprocated it makes people feel good about themselves and

confident and committed in their relationships. You feel lonely because you want that closeness. A study by the University of Nevada asked 248 people what they did to show commitment to their partner. The thing that came out on top? Providing affection, such as hugs and kisses and saying 'I love you.' Women in this study said they gave more affection than men did, but the difference was barely significant. Compliments weren't mentioned, although fidelity as a way of showing commitment was highly popular. Other studies show the importance of talking to each other openly about how you feel about things. If you can't talk to each other that would be more worrying than his inability to hug.

There's evidence that the more affectionate you are, the more it's reciprocated, so don't give up. Keep cuddling and snuggling up – start on the sofa and don't make any sudden moves. You need to take the lead in a non-critical way and explain how you feel about him as a lover and what you need in a relationship. Let him know that although you love him, you're lonely. Don't be critical, but do be clear about what you're asking him to do. You may need to look at getting some professional help with the sex, although many books provide exercises to help relaxation and responsiveness in bed. Perhaps you wish you'd met someone as affectionate as you are but you haven't, so you can either leave this man you love or try again.

ALPHA MALE ALERT

I've been in a long-distance relationship for a year and a half with a guy I really admire. He's intelligent and attractive but he's such an alpha male. I love chatting; I'm into the arts. But he's an engineer who cares more about football than talking to me. Obviously he's never said one word about his emotions, he snaps that he's 'not a girl' and, though I sense that he cares for me, he's never said anything. The solution is probably to move on and find a guy who really communicates. Is there any hope?

There should always be hope, whatever disaster you're facing, but more than hope, you want a chat. Now, to many women alpha males are very attractive, even when they are engineers. These men are dominant (as are the alpha males in animal groups) and have the pick of womankind. Women, however, are generally sensible enough to look for other attributes in long-term relationships, such as compassion, support, intimacy, love and security, according to most research. An example of this research is a study in the *Journal of Personality and Social Psychology* that asked 751 college students for the qualities they most wanted in partners. Attributes such as being hostile and dismissive (as in barking 'I'm not a girl!') did not rate highly. The study showed that people are attracted to others who share their attitudes, but what made for happy relationships were similar personality traits. If you are a chatty extrovert and he won't talk, then the odds are probably against you. If you want intimacy and he doesn't, then you're both going to get cross. In this age of emotional incontinence, refusing to emote can seem rather refreshing. But not when you're trying to establish some basic level of intimacy.

If you are fundamentally different, then maybe there is less optimism than you might be hoping for. A study in the *Proceedings of the National Academy of Sciences* asked 978 men and women (aged eighteen to twenty-four) to rate ten attributes in a mate and then rank themselves for each one. They included wealth, family commitment and fidelity. People who thought an attribute mattered also ranked themselves highly in that same category. The study was a 'what if' rather than a real-life trial, but it suggests that people pick people who are like them.

Some people deliberately avoid intimacy because they don't want to need other people or because they are afraid to. They may choose partners who are like them, who they can keep a safe distance from. There are many research papers linking an avoidance of intimacy to insecure relationships in childhood. You can't psychoanalyse his early relationships, but you can let him know you won't reject him should he choose to tell you how he feels. Having a supportive relationship (that includes sex) with someone has been shown to improve people's mental and physical health and can right some of the wrongs experienced in childhood. Despite what he says, he's likely to be happier if he talks like a girl sometimes.

You ask if your man can become less of an alpha male. Will he change? He may if he wants to, but should you even try? Other men can and do talk and will even say 'I love you' sometimes. Your guy may care for you, but you're saying that's not enough. Put in a concerted effort, and if it fails then consider increasing the length of your long distance.

GONE FOR GOOD?

I've been living with my boyfriend for two years, but he's in a band and often away. He's said he wants some space to see how he feels about the relationship. He's taken some of his things. But on the phone he says he misses me. Is he likely to come back?

Do you want him back? It sounds like he's forgotten that a relationship involves two people and has made a unilateral decision about what he wants. You must be wondering what that space he wants looks like. Is it in his head or some other woman's bed?

You hope he'll have a change of heart, I imagine, but the research suggests most break-ups are for good. A study in the *Journal of Marriage and Family* in 2003 found that only a third of relationships that break up get back together and those that do tend to be the more established ones, with children and shared mortgages. If you are under thirty, the long term reconciliation rate is 1 in 10.

No one can predict what will happen to you – these are just the odds found in various studies, some of which were carried out on university students (you may be older and the results less applicable) – but the statistics are probably starker than you'd expect. Why shouldn't your ex change his mind? He says he misses you, and he hasn't changed his phone number. Unfortunately, the evidence is that leaving is less a physical and more an emotional act. When someone leaves they've usually wanted to do so for months. He won't have woken up one morning and wanted out.

Research in the *Journal of Personality and Social Psychology* from Texas University shows a clear pattern in the death of a relationship. Your boyfriend will have thought about how much he gets out of the relationship, if it has a future and, I'm sorry to say, how easy it will be to find someone else. He will have rehearsed his arguments for leaving you in his head and with his friends. Downplaying his uncertainty makes it easier for him to leave and keeps a foot in the door in case he changes his mind or wants to have sex with you again.

So if you are in the majority of couples who don't get back together you will need to get over him. The mess and sadness of breaking up is not a terminal condition. The research shows that once you know he's gone for good you'll be less upset.

There is no clear evidence on how long it takes to get over someone. Some psychologists say it's a month for every year you've been together. Most of us will know people who seem to recover much faster. Your boyfriend will have been at least a few months ahead of you in deciding it was over; now you need to catch up.

If you wonder if he's hurting as much as you – he isn't. Even if he says 'I feel terrible,' he doesn't feel as bad as you do. The Texas study shows that the person who is left feels worse because they didn't have a choice. But that's not to say that in six months you won't be the happier one.

GULLIBLE OR GUTTED?

*My husband came home from a business trip two months
ago and told me he's gay. We've been married quite happily
for five years, always had sex, so I was devastated when he
told me. We're getting divorced – quite amicably (and I had
a negative HIV test which reassured me). But I'm sure my
friends don't believe me when I say I didn't know. Am I
stupid not to have noticed anything?*

Most women whose husbands come out have no idea they
were gay. Much of the research in this area has been carried
out by Amity Pierce Buxton, whose husband came out as
gay after twenty-five years of marriage. Buxton, who lives
in San Francisco, realized there wasn't much support (her
friends were embarrassed and so was she), so she set up the
Straight Spouse Network. It now has over sixty-five branches
worldwide, including one in the UK. She's the world expert,
having interviewed 11,000 gay and straight spouses and
published research in a book, *The Other Side of the Closet*, and
in academic journals such as the *Journal of Homosexuality*.

Her research shows that most women, like you, are shattered
when their husbands tell them they're gay. If you haven't
already, you'll go through a painful grief process, feeling
deceived, angry and shocked before accepting you've lost the
partner and future you thought you had. Buxton found that
while some women think the infidelity is worse because it's
with a man, others feel better because there's nothing they
could have done about it. In Buxton's surveys one third of

couples divorce straight away, another third split after a year and the rest stay together, usually in open marriages.

Your friends are wrong if they think you must have known. A study of twenty-one women married to homosexual or bisexual men, carried out by the University of Pennsylvania in the *Journal of Homosexuality*, found that only five suspected their husband might be attracted to men. This was a small study (it's not easy to find women in this situation) but a useful one because it asked women in detail what their relationships had been like. Most said they'd had good sex lives and had happy marriages. And although many felt, looking back, their husbands had become distant and gone off sex over the years, they suspected affairs with other women – not men. There were no pink neon signs – other research shows that gay married men can be actively homophobic in an attempt to hide their sexuality. All of the women felt anger and grief that was made worse by feeling deceived and stupid for not guessing the truth. Most found out by their husbands telling them directly.

You might want to ask your husband why he married you. Buxton's research shows that even now some gay men marry women because they want family life and children. They may also fall intellectually in love with a woman while wanting sex with men. Many couples in your situation stay friends because this companionable love remains.

Buxton estimates that 1 to 2 per cent of marriages have one gay spouse. This is backed up by older studies (such as one in the *Social Problems Journal*) that find similar rates across Europe. So it isn't uncommon and you're not stupid – it's a devastating revelation.

IN THE GENES?

My girlfriend and I are thinking of getting married. We've been together for five years and I'd like us to get married before we have kids. My parents have been happily married for thirty years. But her parents got divorced when she was twelve and she's worried this makes it more likely that we'll get divorced. Does it?

I hate to say this, but your girlfriend's right. The research is clear that if you have divorced parents, this increases your own chances of getting divorced. Risk factors can often be hard to quantify – but sadly not in this case. A large US study of more than 2,000 people followed up for over twenty years found that the chances of a couple getting divorced increase by nearly 70 per cent if the wife's parents had split up. If the parents of both the husband and wife divorced, their own risk of doing so increased by 190 per cent. Other studies seem to confirm this.

As you might expect, researchers have tried to figure out why divorce might be, as they say, 'transmitted across generations'. It's not just one generation either. There's a study from Pennsylvania State University of 691 families showing that divorce is more likely in couples whose grandparents got divorced. But these statistics are not the death knell for your marriage prospects. They can give you a forecast of the general but not your own specific risk. On the plus side, forewarned is forearmed.

You can probably guess the theories behind these patterns of divorce. (If not, ask your girlfriend about her parent's divorce.) The US studies and many others show that it's how the parents behave to each other that casts the shadow over the marriages of subsequent generations. The six key behaviours that will have messed up someone's grandparents', parents' and their own chances of marital bliss are being jealous, domineering, angry, critical, moody and not talking to their spouse. These behaviours upset their children, who grow up without learning that couples should support each other and resolve issues in an amicable fashion. These studies do take into account how the children are parented: you can be a better parent than you are a spouse (but conflict in relationships doesn't do much for children). But it seems that children copy how their parents got on with each other, rather than how they were nurtured themselves. The children of parents who fought their way to the divorce courts, grow up, not surprisingly, to be pessimistic about lifelong relationships and fairly enthusiastic about divorce once the honeymoon period is over. They are less likely to trust and commit to relationships. They will not have seen their parents get over the bad times, or handle conflict in constructive ways. The divorce is actually incidental: the research suggests that it's the damage done beforehand that affects the adult relationships of the children involved.

Even amicable divorces increase the risk of children from these families getting divorced. It's not clear if children who grow up with parents who are unhappy but don't split up have an increased risk of divorce – but they are more likely to have unhappy relationships themselves.

So back to you. There are many children of divorced parents who have strong marriages. Marital success is predicated on many things, not just your family history. Your girlfriend's reticence may be because she suspects she has problems with trust and commitment, but you don't, and together you may have the resilience to have a long and happy marriage. And if it all goes pear-shaped you can always blame your in-laws.

THIRD TIME LUCKY?

I am about to marry a lovely man who is everything my first husband wasn't. He talks to me, we do things with my children as a family and should have a great future together. The only thing I worry about is that he's been married twice before (he has two children). Is he more likely to get divorced again, this time from me?

Does practice make perfect? Sadly not, if what you're practising is marriage. Each year over 40 per cent of weddings are remarriages, a doubling of the rate of thirty years ago, according to One Plus One, a UK research organization for couples and families. Unfortunately, these remarriages may be a triumph of optimism over realism; nearly half of all second marriages fail and nearly 60 per cent of third marriages do too. This does not mean that your marriage will not be a triumph, but statistically it is more likely to fail than your first marriage and his second one.

Why should this be? Research in the *Journal of Marriage and Family* suggests that remarried spouses are quicker to criticize and get cross with their partners than those in first marriages.

Most disagreements (and there are more than in first marriages) are about stepchildren, covering such unsolvable problems as discipline, rules and the amount of money spent on them. Remarried couples get on worse when both have children because there is even more to argue about. 'You treat your children differently from mine,' is the signature tune of many reconstituted families. People who remarry may be also more impulsive and unrealistic about how relationships work, seeing divorce as a ready solution to problems. Some people (well, most of us) not only don't learn from their mistakes, but also take them to their next relationship, where they once again cause trouble.

But there is some evidence that remarriages are more equal in how decisions are made and housework distributed. According to a survey of nearly 2,000 people by the University of Texas, despite the disagreements that seem to occur, remarriages that don't end quickly in divorce are almost as happy as first marriages (when the whole length of the marriages are compared).

So remarriages can be happy and most research suggests that people who are married are better off emotionally and financially than those who are single or divorced (unless your marriage is really, chronically miserable). Most people who have divorced do go on to have further relationships in the expectation that they'll be happy. You seem to have found someone who has qualities that you badly wanted and missed in your first marriage, which bodes well.

For you and your children's sake you need to make sure that your odds of success are as high as possible. If you haven't probed before, now's the time to do it. Discuss how you plan to bring up your children, in particular who will discipline them, and how. Ask him how you will resolve disputes together. Better still: although love is a wonderful thing, check if he's got any money – weddings are costly but divorces and their aftermath are much more expensive.

Sex Lives

TRI-WEEKLY

I've been living with my girlfriend for about two years and we get on really well. The problem is that we don't have much sex. When we first started going out, we had sex every day and it was great – now we can go days without it. Is this normal – does it happen to everyone?

What is it about sex that makes people worry if they're having a 'normal' amount? Mostly, and in this case, the answer is yes. You and your girlfriend clearly used to have a good sex life (assuming there was quality to go with quantity). The problem is that nearly all couples have less sex the longer they're together. Researchers partly blame a process called 'habituation', a fancy way of saying that sex (with your partner) loses its novelty value. After the initial uncertainty and excitement, the sex in your relationship may be pushed into the background by pressures at work, a tedious commute or a long-running television series.

It's hard to benchmark your own sex life. Fortunately it's done for us by surveys such as the Sexual Attitudes and Lifestyles Survey, the largest ever done in the UK, which allows us a degree of voyeurism into the sex lives of others. It asked nearly 19,000 people how often they had sex. Both men and women in their mid twenties to mid thirties had sex on average eight to nine times a month. But once they'd been with their partners for over two years it fell to six times. So if you do go some days without sex this really is normal. People under twenty-five have sex around eleven times a month but even they have it less often the longer they've been in a couple.

The average disguises a wide range – in most studies from no sex to forty-five times a month. The amount of sex you have as a couple is set by you, not by the national average, nor by what your friends are doing (should they tell you). A study from the Faculty of Arts and Sciences in New Brunswick in Canada in the *Journal of Sex Research* found that in the first year couples develop a pattern for how often they have sex. And if they were above the average then, they will continue to be so, even after two years. So although mortgages and having kids are great contraceptives, a couple with both may still have more sex than the young child-free couple across the street. Although it seems unlikely.

You may not have negotiated with your girlfriend just how much sex you want because it isn't a spontaneous and sexy thing to do. If you want more sex there are numerous studies, as well as common sense, that say you should talk about it. You may have to make a conscious effort to set aside time for sex. The New Brunswick study found that taking turns to initiate sex made couples more satisfied with their sex lives, as did talking to each other about what they liked during sex. The study showed it's best to take a direct rather than euphemistic approach. Don't say, 'Let's have an early night,' because that's exactly what you'll get.

TRY WEEKLY

I've lost interest in sex. I really love my partner and have been with him for twelve years (we have two kids, who are eight and ten), but over the last year I've lost my sex drive. He's still attractive to me, but if he starts something it's a real effort to become aroused. I could probably do without sex altogether but know he couldn't. Is it normal to lose interest in sex? Would Viagra help me?

It's normal to lose interest in sex, but rather inconvenient if you're in a relationship. Many women say that once they've had children they go off sex (preferring sleep) or find it more challenging to get aroused. Surveys show that people do have sex when they don't want it, but when it becomes a huge effort this isn't an option. A study in the *Journal of the American Medical Association* surveyed 1,749 women between eighteen and fifty-nine and found that 43 per cent of them (compared with 31 per cent of the 1,410 men surveyed) had problems with sex – mostly related to loss of desire and arousal. But this figure has been hotly debated as too high – women were asked questions about lack of desire, anxiety about sexual performance and difficulties with lubrication for two months or more. If they said yes to any one question they were classified as having sexual problems. While pharmaceutical companies might like a woman's loss of interest in sex to be a medical problem, it really isn't a disease and it is not helpful to think of it as such. More realistically, an *Observer* poll of 1,027 people by ICM Research found that only 19 per cent said their sex drive was low or very low.

There are some medical reasons for losing interest in sex, for example the pill, depression, alcohol, diabetes, anything that makes sex painful, the menopause, quite a few medicines and stress. But most often a change in desire is a reasonable response to the challenges of life. For example, a study by the National Institutes for Health in the US found that women on low incomes were up to two thirds more likely to have sexual problems than other women. Even without financial stress, many women find it hard to order their lives so that sex gets a time slot. In the long list of women's jobs – mother, worker, friend, daughter – lover (unfortunately) comes last.

Desire and arousal have complex biological pathways that start in the brain. Viagra (which is not licensed for women) may get more blood to the genitals, but so does more foreplay and even the anticipation of foreplay. You have to do the cheesy stuff of making time for sex, avoiding the mundane (not in bed, legs up with the lights out) and using music as a diversion to relieve inhibitions. You will need to masturbate more, use vibrators, massage, stimulate orally and fantasize. You don't need to feel aroused to start. Trust that your interest will increase as you get going. But you will need, above all, to talk to your partner. Not only about sex, what you do and don't like, but how close you are and how your relationship is doing. Is your man doing his share around the house? There's considerable research showing that women over thirty feel more sexual interest in a partner who's handy with a vacuum cleaner. How convenient is that? Do you know how you're each doing at work? It's a myth that sex is a natural activity that anyone can do. After the first flush of youth it's a game of skill. If you don't want a sexless relationship you'll both have to work at regaining your interest.

TRY WEAKLY

I am engaged to a man I met two years ago. We have the same understanding of how to live, but there is one big catch: the sexual chemistry is not fulfilling. My sex drive is higher than his, and the few times we do have sex rarely lead to orgasm for me. We have talked about it many times; his point is he just doesn't care about sex that much. He has mentioned that he thinks sex is dirty. Can I marry someone with whom I have this sort of issue?

You shouldn't marry someone who you have sexual problems with just yet, because the evidence is overwhelming that the difficulties cause conflict and unhappiness in relationships, and you sound pretty miserable already. Sexual problems are common and his type sounds like it could be hypoactive sexual desire (HSD). A research paper in the *British Medical Journal* found that out of 500 men visiting their GPs, 1 in 5 had a sexual problem. Difficulties with erections and loss of desire were the most common.

Sexual mythology would have us believe that men don't ever lose their desire for sex, but they do. There are many reasons for this: illness (up to a third are caused by physical factors or side effects of medicines), stress and sometimes a long-standing dislike of sex or lack of real physical attraction between couples. A survey of over 800 people by netdoctor. com found that a quarter had been brought up to think sex is 'dirty' (not in a good way), so your fiancé is not unusual in his negativity. Sexual mythology would also have us believe that sexual chemistry makes sex effortless – it doesn't – so don't convince yourself that a lack of this ephemeral substance is to blame. However uncertain you are of the cause, be sure that it will cause problems in your relationship. A study of seventy-two couples in the *Archives of Sexual Behavior* found that those with the greatest differences in desire had the most unhappy relationships.

People with HSD don't tend to have sexual fantasies or feel much need to have sex. They may not understand how desire works and think it comes on like a light rather than developing as you're having sex. They may not associate feeling intimate with wanting sex, believing that only hardcore erotic feelings should initiate sex. People with HSD are often emotionally distanced, although this may be the effect rather than the cause of their problems. You sound rather detached from him too, and he may need as much love and understanding as you can bear to give him. Sex can bring you closer together, but you sometimes have to be intimate in the first place to want to have it.

So this is not about the quantity but the quality of sex and may not even be just about him. Sexual problems tend to involve two people, and in a third of couples where HSD is an issue the other partner will have their sexual difficulties too. The fact that you are compatible in other ways is encouraging and may make you both motivated to sort out your sexual problems.

You've got a lot to work out and you will need help. Couple counselling (or an approachable family doctor) is a good start, as sex may only be part of the problem. It's certainly a better place to start working on your relationship than at your wedding reception.

DREAM ON

My partner enjoys telling me about his sexual fantasies. They often involve someone who isn't me, which irritates me. Is this something men do more than women?

Most people have sexual fantasies, but they shouldn't feel compelled to share them. Fantasies are private thoughts and can be sexually inhibiting as well as liberating. Taking offence at a fantasy, however, invests it with too much meaning. It's just a thought (unless it really is depraved, in which case phone the police).If it's about a friend of yours they'd be best to keep it to themselves, as this type of fantasy goes down particularly badly. But it is still just a fantasy.

There are hundreds of books on sexual fantasies, so the subject certainly generates interest. And it isn't a male preserve: the American sexologist Nancy Friday has made a living from her bestselling books on female fantasies, called *My Secret Garden* and *Forbidden Flowers* (get the theme?).

Studies show what you'd expect, though: there are differences between the sexes, with men having more fantasies. A study by researchers at the University of Vermont of nearly 350 people whose ages ranged from eighteen to seventy (all either students or faculty at another university in New England, so this wasn't a study representative of most people) found that nearly all of the men in their sample and 80 per cent of women had sexual fantasies about people who weren't their partner. So men do it more, but so do most women, which is interesting as nearly half of respondents in a *New York Times* poll in 2000 said that it was 'not okay' to fantasize about having sex with someone else.

Women were more likely than men in the Vermont study to fantasize about an ex partner – although these fantasies were uncommon. The longer people had been in a relationship, and the more partners they'd had, the more likely they were to fantasize about someone else. The average length of time people in the study had been in relationships was nine years and four months. So you may not like it, but it's normal and you shouldn't feel jealous. The study did find that people who fantasized about other people were more likely to have been unfaithful to their partner. But that doesn't prove one causes the other – so don't get cross. Unfaithfulness in this study was also broadly defined – it included kissing, which may not be everyone's idea of full-blown infidelity.

Men and women may not be aroused by each other's fantasies because their fantasies may be different. This is shown in other studies that suggest that men's fantasies focus more on the act of having sex, with less emotion and romance, than women's do. A study in the *Journal of Sex Research* from the University of California asked 162 people between the ages of twenty-one and forty-five to write sexual fantasies (as part of their research into links between power in sexual fantasies and the acceptance of myths about rape) and found that men's fantasies were more explicit, involved more sexual partners and had themes of dominance. But men were also likely to fantasize about their partners being easily pleased and aroused. So your partner is also likely to have fantasies in which you're having a sexually amazing time. You may need to remind him that in real life more effort is needed to achieve these fantasies – and they're really the only ones you want to hear about.

ADDICTED TO LOVE

My friend's boyfriend is continually unfaithful to her – one of us even caught him having sex with someone else at a party. However, he's now told her he's a sex addict. He says he loves her and will join a sex addicts' support group. Isn't 'sex addiction' a pathetic excuse for his inability to be faithful? Shouldn't my friend just leave him?

It will be hard for your friend to stay with her boyfriend if he keeps having sex with other people. Most people really don't like that. Whether or not the cause is his 'addiction' to sex is more debatable. The field of sex addiction is a hotbed of academic argument, with some people saying that it is like drug addiction, others that it is compulsive behaviour (akin to obsessively washing your hands for hours) and a third school that it's a form of behaviour that's impulsive or out of control. What no one disputes is that this preoccupation with sex damages relationships. People who claim to be addicted to sex will say that their everyday life is devoted to having sex. They can't stop looking for ever more partners (including paying for sex) or more pornography or both. It makes people sexualize ordinary events, use others for sex in a selfish way and increasingly feel disgusted with themselves. Instead of going to work, seeing their partner, meeting up with friends, or doing their tax return, they will be looking for or having sex, with themselves if no one else is around.

However, sexuality is such a variable thing that the condition is also likely to overlap with the behaviour of relatively normal (albeit sometimes sexually selfish) people. Some people are highly sexual and like to have orgasms several times a day. However, self-confessed sex addicts don't like what they're doing and may feel compelled to have sex when they feel depressed or anxious. Sex is not about pleasure for them but about filling an emotional void. Forgive this short simplistic description – there are textbooks for the really interested, but, unlike abnormal sexual stuff, like touching up strangers, there's no agreed psychiatric definition.

There are few UK studies, but a paper in the journal *Postgraduate Medicine* puts the rate of sex addiction at 3 to 6 per cent. There is more research from America which shows the same rates. Surveys show that some people having out-of-control sex were abused as children – between one and two thirds (although this abuse is not defined). Up to two thirds of people having out of control sex have other addictions.

Treatments vary and are contentious, such as a twelve-step programme adapted from the successful one from Alcoholics Anonymous but with abstinence for only thirty to ninety days (it includes a masturbation ban that online discussion forums suggest is usually broken). Total abstinence from sex would be somewhat limiting in life. A combination of drugs, sometimes to treat depression and anxiety, and talking therapies can help, but there isn't a cure and people do remain at risk of repeating their behaviours. It's up to your friend if she can stay with him – some couples do manage – but she will need to have huge reserves of understanding, forgiveness and supportive friends.

SEX TOYS

My wife and I are either side of fifty and love each other very much, but our sex life – particularly when our children were younger – has always had its highs and lows. Two years ago in an attempt to rekindle our sex life I bought her a vibrator, which I had hoped we could use together. However, I'm now worried that the idea may have backfired on me, as I know she uses it but seems to want to make love with me even less frequently.

How nice of you to get her a vibrator. Unfortunately, she's found out (presuming she hadn't used one before) that it's much easier to have an orgasm with a vibrator than with another human being. In fact, for many women, whatever they use, it's easier to have an orgasm on their own.

Contrary to popular belief, people over fifty want to and do have sex. A study on sexuality in 500 older women by researchers at the Royal Brisbane and Women's Hospital in Australia found that over half of them between the ages of forty and eighty were having sex, often a few times a month.

But the news wasn't all good, especially for Australian men. The researchers found that 56 per cent of women who were sexually active without a partner had an orgasm every time they masturbated compared with only 24 per cent of women having sex with a partner. This may seem obvious – the former is not an activity people usually start without finishing – but it suggests that some men are not as careful or skilful in stimulating their partners as they might be. No one is saying that ordinary mortals can provide the intense stimulation of a vibrator – although a study from the City University of New York into the quality and speed to orgasm comparing different types of vibrator still found a variation in reaching an orgasm from 20 seconds to an hour. But a partner should offer a more well-rounded, intimate sexual experience (a vibrator can't be romantic), and it is this that you would hope your wife would want. What you need to ask (yourself but her in particular) is whether you have satisfying sex with each other.

As women and men get older, their desire for sex can tail off a bit. They may feel less attractive or have health problems that make sex more of an effort. After the menopause, sex is just harder for women sometimes; it takes longer for blood to get to the right bits and for lubrication to kick in. Sex toys eliminate the need to feel desire, as all you have to do is switch them on, but there's a risk in that the instant gratification is more mechanical than emotional.

All couples have sex lives that ebb and flow, but you need to ask how emotionally close you are now (after all these years) and how affectionate you are to each other. The same issues that affect the sex lives of younger couples apply to older ones too. If your sex life has become boring or you aren't sexually fulfilling each other, or you are no longer emotionally close, you need to find out or you'll never dislodge that vibrator. If you're intimate enough to buy her a vibrator in the first place you should be able to do that.

JUST FOR THE CELIBATE

My husband and I have stopped having sex. I'm not sure why we have embraced celibacy, but our marriage has been sexless for about a year (I know he's not having an affair). We've both been struggling at work and with our teenage children, so I'm not sure I miss it. He doesn't seem bothered, but how can our relationship last if we never have sex together again?

If you don't know why you've become a celibate couple you can try the usual reasons. Dr Denise Donnelly's study of 6,029 married people in the *Journal of Sex Research* found that couples were less likely to have sex if they were unhappy (hard to know which came first, it's reciprocal), had small children and didn't do much together. Infidelity, illness, concerns about appearance and getting older can also put people off sex, as can pregnancy. All things considered it's amazing that couples ever have sex. But they do, and when celibacy usurps sex it is rarely by mutual decision, or a matter that is fully discussed. When it does happen it usually leaves one person feeling rejected, frustrated and unhappy.

You need to work out if you're what one self-help website calls an 'incel'. This is short for 'involuntary celibate' (incelsite.

com). You would qualify if you wanted sex, in this case with your husband, but couldn't have it, either because 'the spark' (that elusive core of modern marriages) had gone or he didn't want it anymore. Or could *he* be the incel and you the one who's okay with no sex? Unfortunately, as you suspect, your relationship may not be okay. Another study by Donnelly of seventy-seven incels in marriages or long-term relationships in the *Journal of Marriage and Family* used a web-based questionnaire to ask people why they stayed in their sexless relationships (defined in this case as no sex for six months). This study was not representative of the general population, because not everyone uses the internet (really they don't) and these people came from an online discussion group. But it's not easy to find incels, so the results are still useful. Over 64 per cent of people said that sex had gradually tailed off for them (from a mixture of tiredness and not being bothered). As a result, around 26 per cent had had affairs, one third had had therapy (but generally didn't feel it helped) and only a third were reconciled to a celibate relationship. Incels spoke of being unhappy and feeling incomplete without sex.

Your relationship may last without sex, but you couldn't bet on it being better. The longer you go without sex the less you miss it – so don't kid yourself it's a considered choice. Donnelly's study found that half the people said their ideal partner was their current one – if only they'd have sex again. Other studies show that most often it's the man who decides to stop having sex, usually without discussing it first and sometimes because it's more difficult for him to have an erection or feel sexually interested. If that's true for you then at least talk to your husband about it and try to rekindle your sex life. It may feel like an enormous effort to start with, but it's so, so much easier in the long run.

IT'S WIDTH NOT LENGTH

I've been worried about my penis being smaller than other blokes' since I was at school, but my girlfriend says I'm mad and it is fine. Statistics suggest it is average, and I've heard thickness rather than length matters to women. Is that true, and can you make a penis bigger?

Lots of men do worry about the size of their penis. But the odds are that you are within the normal range given by one study or other. A study by Lifestyles Condom Co. of 300 men found that two thirds of penises were between 5.1 and 6.2 inches long when erect. The penises were measured by nurses rather than by the men themselves, so this study is more likely to be accurate than those that rely on men doing it themselves. The erect penis is not easy to measure, but you can try to do it by using a tape measure from the base of the penis where it touches the pubic bone (press in especially if you have a paunch there) to the tip. Some experts suggest that measuring a penis by stretching it when flaccid is an even more accurate guide to how long it will be when erect. The Kinsey Institute's *New Report on Sex* says that the average man's erect penis is 5 to 7 inches long and has a circumference of 4 to 6 inches. The rule of thumb is that an erect penis is twice the size of a flaccid one.

Men seem to underestimate the size of their own penis and overestimate the size of everyone else's. This is because you look down on your penis, literally, but sideways at other men's. Look at yours sideways in the mirror and your worry may evaporate; it's instantly bigger. A study in the *International*

Journal of Impotence Research in Italy of sixty-seven men asking for surgical enhancement found that none of them had abnormally small penises. Once shown where their penises stood on a graph (in the normal range) forty-eight men (72 per cent) went away happily but nineteen (28 per cent) still wanted surgery. The researchers offered psychosexual counselling first, but only eleven agreed (the surgeons would not do surgery without counselling first) and the study doesn't say how many men eventually had the operation (although considerably less than the sixty-seven who initially asked for it). Studies show that even men with true micropenises (which affects less than 1 in 200 men) have good sex lives. Surgery is unlikely to help any man whose penis is a normal size anyway.

The sex-research pioneers William Masters and Virginia E. Johnson said size didn't matter because the vagina accommodates what is offered. A study in the *British Medical Journal* of magnetic resonance imaging of couples having sex shows the base of the penis taking up a lot of the room (thereby helping clitoral stimulation) and the penis bending into a boomerang shape. Length may look more enticing (too long and it can look threatening) but the reality is that most of it isn't needed. Girth, however, does seem to be important. A small study of fifty women aged between eighteen and twenty-five by the University of Texas-Pan American found that forty-five said width was more important than length.

If you still want to know if there is anything that makes penises longer, the answer is no, not really. You can cut ligaments so the penis dangles more (but isn't really longer), inject fat into the penis which can make it lumpy, and wear frames that extend the penis. Suction pumps make penises swollen but sore. There are other surgical techniques, but results are mediocre and the procedures carry some risk.

As for women, they don't really care. Better to invest in some thoughtful foreplay techniques than fret about penile enhancement. A penis is not nearly as important as the thoughtful and skilful lover attached to it.

SAVE SEX

I am seventeen years old and most of my friends have had sex. I don't feel ready to lose my virginity. My mum says that when she was young they waited longer before having sex. Isn't it better for a relationship to wait?

Sexual attitudes have changed since your mum's time. The National Survey of Sexual Attitudes and Lifestyles from 2000 finds that the average age for people to have sex for the first time now is sixteen for both men and women. The Economic and Social Research Council (ESRC) says that the median age for the first time people have sex has fallen roughly four years in the past forty years. So people did used to wait longer, especially before the pill came along.

Conversely, people now wait longer to become more committed. Once upon a time, sex did mean commitment (and I am not saying that's a good thing, okay?). Over the past forty years, the ESRC estimates that the time from having sex to living with someone (anyone – not who you first had sex with) has risen from one to four years for women and four to seven years for men. The downside of earlier sexual activity is the rise in sexually transmitted diseases (think about the risk today of chlamydia) and Britain's propensity for teenage pregnancy and high teenage abortion rates. So arguably we're not very good at having sex earlier – one reason for waiting.

Also, sex, like most things, gets better with practice, so it's unlikely to be a great success from the start. The research shows that however cool it is to see sex as a recreational activity, it is usually best with someone you know, like, trust, can talk to and be un-cool with. You may not need to wait long to find someone like that, but you'll have a better time if you do.

Call me old-fashioned, but I don't see why there's a rush. If peer-group pressure becomes unbearable, you can always be vague – it's not uncommon for people to exaggerate their sexual experience. A MORI poll for the *Observer* showed that out of 1,618 people, 18 per cent of women waited over two months before having sex in a relationship (but only half the sample answered – most saying it varied). In your mum's time a study from East Carolina University of 555 students found that three quarters of the women felt petting should wait until the fourth date, while almost one third of men thought it should occur on the first date. Things generally went slower back then.

The ESRC report says that women are twice as likely as men to regret the first time they had sex and three times as likely as men to say they were less willing than their partners. So it's perfectly sensible not to have sex before you are ready. Sex is so ubiquitous that it may seem strange to a potential boyfriend that there's anything to need to wait for. But that doesn't mean you can't wait if you want to.

NEUROTIC EROTIC

I caught my boyfriend of nine months looking at porn on the internet the other night. I asked him how often he did this and he said not much, but I'm not sure if I believe him. I was really upset, but now I think maybe I'm overreacting and that lots of men do this. Do they?

Lots of men do look at porn online, but that doesn't mean you can't get upset if your boyfriend is one of them. You should know, however, that it is a common male pastime. A survey by Nielsen NetRatings shows that 1 in 4 men aged twenty-five to forty-nine has visited an adult porn site in the past month. Other surveys put the percentage at more like 60 per cent. Ask men and they will say they're surprised these figures are so low. Who wouldn't take a peek if it's freely available?

Porn on the internet can vary from the type found in men's magazines to the more nasty stuff – I'm assuming he was looking at mainstream porn, and some women are fairly relaxed about their men doing this. A study of 100 women whose partners used pornography, published in the *Journal of Sex and Marital Therapy*, found that most weren't bothered but that one quarter to a third were distressed by it. These women felt their partners had been unfaithful to them by looking at pornography, especially when the women they were lusting over had 40DD breasts. They worried that in comparison they were overweight and unsexy (and who wouldn't be?) and hence not good enough. Some took their insecurity one step further and asked themselves if their partners used pornography because they themselves were so undesirable (the research shows this isn't true – most men who use it do so because it's available). They also worried that their partner used pornography because they found their sex lives unfulfilling. Women with feminist tendencies, who felt that porn objectifies women, wondered if this was how their partners really felt about them.

But Dr Ana Bridges, who carried out the study, thinks that most men who use porn do so just because it's there. It most likely says nothing about how they feel about their partners or their relationships; they just like the visual stimulation. Bridges estimates that in a quarter of relationships porn-use may mean something, but it's hard to say what.

Bearing in mind that it may or not mean something, try to work out why you're upset and take a practical rather than moral approach. People vary in all sorts of ways, including in what they find arousing. Is your relationship otherwise happy? Are you having enough sex (as men who use porn can get lazy and just have sex with themselves), and is it good sex? You need to talk to your partner and let him know you're upset. He may be able to convince you that it's fine for him to use porn or to negotiate on his use. For example, you may be okay if he uses it when you're out but not when you're in the next room (and hence available). Be clear about what you agree but don't monitor his use because it will end in tears.

The Nielsen NetRatings survey showed that women also liked visual stimulation, with 1.4 million a year looking at online porn. Men may be as unhappy as women about their partners doing this. Other surveys show that just as many men as women feel insecure when their partner looks at porn. Bridges suggests that couple take pictures of each other for visual stimulation, but only if they trust each other to never post them on the internet.

BORN TO USE PORN?

I enjoy pornography. I'd really like my girlfriend to watch it with me, because I think it would make our sex more exciting. She doesn't seem that interested. I've watched pornography with other girlfriends. How can I get her to try it?

It's an individual thing, liking or not liking pornography. Most pornography is made for and marketed to men, and studies show that men start using porn earlier than women and are more enthusiastic about it. Feminists have argued either that porn exploits women or that it arouses them but they're too repressed to admit it. What's certain is that discussions about porn are usually loaded with morality.

Figures for the use of pornography by women are not terribly robust. Dr Clarissa Smith, author of the book *One for the Girls* and senior lecturer in media and cultural studies at the University of Sunderland, says that 40 per cent is an accepted estimate. This is based on a Nielsen NetRatings survey of women's use of pornography on the web in 2006, while a review article in *Archives of Sexual Behavior* says that out of the 40 million adults accessing pornography websites annually, 72 per cent are men and 28 per cent women. Smith's own research, interviewing women who bought *For Women* (a porn magazine for women), found that they mostly looked at the magazine on their own: they didn't want to be distracted while they were being aroused. Smith says that women shouldn't be coerced into watching porn just because their partner wants to, but if you can interest your girlfriend, try female directors, such as Candida Royalle and Ana Span, who specialize in porn films for couples. Span's view is that women want better-looking men and more soap opera in their porn. They also like their porn stars to have better clothes and accessories.

The most rigorous research in this area has been carried out in Denmark, a country unencumbered by pornography guilt. Gert Martin Hald's study of 688 men and women (aged eighteen to thirty) in the *Archives of Sexual Behavior* found that almost all men and 80 per cent of women had used porn at least once – 50 per cent of the women in the past month. Hald's definition of pornography was that it had to include 'explicit exposure or description of the genitals', but it also had to show actual intercourse; browsing *Playboy* or *Playgirl* didn't count. Women were more likely to watch pornography with a partner than on their own – twice as likely as men were. Hald's view is that it isn't shame that stops women being as turned on by porn as men: they just think about sex differently. Most porn, he says, is used by men to masturbate and shows an easily available woman that they don't have to invest in at all. Thin plots about pizza delivery men turning up and getting it on demand usually do more for men than women.

Once you've asked your girlfriend to watch porn with you, you shouldn't keep asking if she says no. It won't be helpful for your sex life to make her feel guilty and repressed. If she isn't interested then you'll have to think of other ways to boost your sex lives. Traditionally, sex with feelings is a winner for women. And you could still dress up as the pizza delivery man.

Surviving Children

BUNDLE OF JOY?

My partner is convinced that having a baby will ruin both our relationship and his life. Is there any evidence to show he could be right? Can the arrival of a baby split apart an otherwise blissfully happy couple?

Couples often think that a baby will make them even more blissful. But they'd be wrong. For most couples babies can be bad news. There's a lot of research on the 'transition to parenthood', and some of it is contradictory. But a meta-analytic study of the quality of relationships after children (in the *Journal of Marriage and Family*), which added up results from ninety studies (covering 31,331 people), found generally that couples with children were less happy than non-parents. Women with children under one were the least happy, only 38 per cent of them having higher than average levels of satisfaction with their relationships compared to 62 per cent who hadn't yet had children. Men didn't show reduced levels of bliss until the second year of the baby's life, although by the time the child was two both men and women were feeling better about their relationships.

The reasons are obvious. Babies deprive you of sleep – which in itself causes conflict. They erode your time together and mess up your sex life, and women still usually bear the brunt of childcare responsibilities and are more likely to feel ground down and resentful (especially if they are combining motherhood with a career). The study also showed that the more children a couple had the less happy they were likely to be. Other studies show that conflict doesn't end when children get past the toddling stage – it's the teenage years that can be the most challenging.

So what's the good news? Well, children do bring joy, and the research, while not conclusive, suggests that on a personal level they make the people who have them more rather than less happy. And if you are a blissful couple to start with it definitely helps. A study in the *Journal of Family Psychology* of eighty-two couples found that those with good relationships were protected from the destructive effects of babies. Couples who weren't critical of each other but gently tried to solve problems together, who were affectionate and in particular where the man helped out, were the happiest after having a baby. This supports the findings from other studies that show parents who compete for their child's attention and undermine each other's parenting are more likely to be unhappy. A big predictor of happiness is whether the decision to have a baby was mutual. So be warned – especially as children don't thrive when their parents are constantly fighting.

I'd hope your relationship can stand a baby. But forewarned is forearmed. The organization One Plus One has an excellent paper called *The Transition to Parenthood – The Magic Moment*, which says that babies tend neither to cause good-quality relationships to deteriorate nor to bring unhappy couples any closer together. They quote some researchers showing an increase in relationship satisfaction of between 18 per cent and 30 per cent when couples become parents. Most importantly, the research shows that couples do better if they know what's coming.

CHANGING MINDS

I would love to have children, but my partner has said that he doesn't want to. I almost wish we'd never discussed it and it had just happened. If I did get pregnant, wouldn't he just come round to the idea?

The trouble is that your partner would have to come round to the baby itself, not just the idea. On the one hand you can curse yourself for bringing the subject up. At least one third of pregnancies in the UK are unplanned according to a study in the *Lancet*, so you could have presented him with a scenario that goes, 'Oh no, the condom must have split,' or 'I should never have taken these antibiotics with my pill.' But on the other hand it's worth knowing how your partner feels about having children. This is because children disrupt relationships. We know this because the research keeps telling us so. A large review of ninety-seven studies with 47,692 people in the *Journal of Marriage and Family* found that 'married with kids' meant less-satisfied relationships than being married without them. However, children are a deterrent to splitting up, at least initially, so this may bias the results. Even so, overall 55 per cent of couples without children had higher than average levels of happiness with their relationship compared with 45 per cent of parents. The extra work, sleep deprivation and loss of freedom all take their toll, however cute the baby is.

So you really did have to ask him how he felt about being a father. Studies show that men can be underwhelmed by having children, expecting to enjoy it much more than they do. Men often feel more anxious about providing for their children financially; so instead of bonding with their baby, you'll find them working inappropriately late in the office.

What the research is quite clear about is that men who do not want a pregnancy (let alone a baby at the end of it) are unlikely to be enthusiastic about it. A study of 6,816 fathers who lived with their babies measured how often they changed nappies, comforted the baby when it cried (nurturing activities), how much they held and tickled the baby (warmth activities) and whether the pregnancy was wanted or not. About 8 per cent of the fathers did not want the pregnancy and 20 per cent wanted it but not just yet, thanks. The study found that having a baby didn't bring fathers round: those that hadn't wanted the baby were much less likely to hold their baby or be affectionate to it.

Fathers are more likely to get involved as children grow up, and some research suggests that they're more involved if they have a son. They are also more involved if their relationship is strong and happy. A relationship is unlikely to be happy if it is built on unilateral decision-making. You need to talk about what having a baby really means – the impact it will have on your lifestyle, ambitions and relationship. It's fair to your

partner and it's fair to the baby you want to have, who would
(I'm guessing) prefer to be wanted by both its parents.

IMPACT OF INFERTILITY

*We're finally giving up trying for a baby after many years
and trying to accept a child-free life. Our infertility was
'unexplained', and we've been through traumatic times but
still stayed together. But what will happen to us now we've
given up the hope of having children? Will our relationship
and lives recover from this?*

Infertility is immensely distressing. The tests and treatment
are stressful and it can take years to grieve for the life you
expected to have. What the research does seem to show,
however, is that couples do survive.

Between 10 and 17 per cent of couples have some infertility
problems, according to a paper in the journal *Human
Reproduction* from researchers at Helsinki University Central
Hospital. Regardless of who has the problem, the research
shows that couples do better when they feel the same way
about their infertility (equally sad, angry or accepting). You
also do better if you tell each other how you feel, but of course
you knew that.

The problem is the time it takes to readjust your lives. A
study in the *Journal of Counselling and Development* of thirty-

seven couples from Canadian cities who stopped treatment, asked how they were coping at ten-monthly intervals. It took up to three years, of exhaustion and hopelessness (the first ten months), frustration and anger (some felt they had put their lives on hold to have children), before they could feel optimistic about life again. Although couples questioned their relationships, many said they'd grown closer. The study was small, however, and didn't say how many couples stayed together.

Being sensitive to each other's feelings is easier said than done if you're crying your eyes out. A study of 420 couples in the journal *Family Relations* who were still having treatment found that women were most distressed when their husbands distanced themselves and men found it hard to cope when their wives kept their feelings to themselves. Couples who were best able to support each other were those who didn't blame themselves or each other for the fertility problems. How you cope will also depend partly on your family's expectations for you and on your feelings about adoption and surrogacy. Infertility organizations suggest joining support groups and couples counselling.

I couldn't find any evidence that infertility increases the risk of divorce. But more importantly neither can Professor Arthur L. Greil, a sociologist and expert in this area from Alfred University in New York. Couples, he tells me, get stressed, but many say their relationships grow stronger. The relationships are as likely to be as happy (and that includes being as sexually fulfilling) as anyone else's – however hard this may be for you to believe right now.

SEASONAL BIRTH DISORDERS

We are trying for a baby. We know we may not be able to engineer exactly when I get pregnant, but, if we could pick a time of year, what's the best month to have a baby?

The answer is that it depends who's asking. The answer for the baby may be different from the one for the woman who's carrying it. Panting in the summer heat with a swollen belly that hides even bigger ankles is uncomfortable for a woman. But on the other hand a study from the University of Southampton that looked at 1,750 men and women born in Hertfordshire over one decade found men born in winter had an increased risk of obesity. You wouldn't want to wish that on your baby, now would you? Figures from the Office for National Statistics show that babies born in winter may also have an increased risk of being stillborn and dying before they're a month old. However, these tragic events are rare, and no one would suggest you avoid a winter birth because of them.

Most research into the 'seasonality' effects of birth doesn't look at whether it's more pleasant to push a buggy through autumnal leaves or spring showers. It looks for more heavyweight things, such as links between birthdays and serious illnesses. Researchers have looked for and found some seasonal links with Parkinson's disease (spring), multiple sclerosis (10 per cent more in May, according to a study in the *British Medical Journal*), epilepsy (winter), brain tumours (January/February), coeliac disease (summer) and risk of suicide (April, May and June). There are many other studies on other diseases, but the strength of most of these associations is not clear and it seems that most months have some theoretical risk attached to them.

A more real worry is that children born late in the school year struggle to keep up with their peers. A study from the Institute of Fiscal Studies confirms this, finding that children born in August do worse in school tests for most of their academic careers and are more likely to drop out at the age of sixteen. This isn't the fault of August but of their relative young age within their year group. At the age of eleven, August-born girls are two thirds more likely than other children to have a diagnosed learning difficulty. As the general secretary of the Association of School and College Leaders in England was quoted as saying, 'You don't do your children any favours by having them in July or August.' But on the other hand the weather is better and you can go for walks.

Office for National Statistics figures show the most common months for babies to be born are May to August, with another peak in September. This ties in nicely with the winter-nights hypothesis, where couples can't watch television night after night and become sufficiently cold and bored to have sex. (Everyone knows that it's not hot weather that makes you sexually insatiable – it just makes you sweaty and bothered.) This pattern of winter sex giving rise to summer births is seen in other European countries. In the Netherlands the organization that collects these figures, Statistics Netherlands, reports that the most common months for babies are July, August and September.

If you do plan when to give birth then you will be being highly organized. This quality alone will stand you in good stead whatever month you have your baby in.

KIDS AS CONTRACEPTIVES

*My husband and I have a two-and-a-half year old and a
six-month old baby (who I still breastfeed). My husband
is unhappy with the amount of sex we have. He says the
average is three times a week, but we should be doing it five
times to make up for lost time (pregnancy, post-birth). I
say leave me alone so I can sleep while there's a chance. I
don't want to ask the other mothers at playgroup, but what's
everyone else doing?*

Most mothers of young children aren't looking for more sex.
They're desperate for sleep, not the chance to catch up on
erotic action they missed out on while either heavily pregnant
or giving birth. The other mothers at playgroup would be
impressed by the amount of sex you're having, because the
average your husband is quoting is not for parents. It's for
childless couples in their early twenties.

The amount of sex that people have varies according to many
things, such as if they're single (less sex), if they've been with
someone a long time (longer usually means less), how old
they are (less over the age of fifty), if they're worried about
anything (who isn't? – and it's less) and if they have children
(less again, when the children are young). The biggest sexual
survey in the UK carried out in the 1990s asked 18,876 people
about their sex lives and on average people under forty have
sex six times a month. The average hides some considerable
variation: for example, couples under twenty-five have sex

eleven times a month (apparently still not enough for your husband).

Having children, especially young ones, undoubtedly reduces a couple's sexual activity. A recent survey of 20,000 parents by the website BabyCenter found that six months after the birth the average was three to five times a month. A study of 570 women and 550 of their partners in the *Journal of Sexual Research* found that couples had sex four to five times a month during pregnancy, stopped for seven weeks afterwards, and then went back to mid-pregnancy levels of sex by the time their babies were four months old. It took a year for them to feel the sex was as good as it had been before the baby arrived. Other studies have found that even after a year up to 95 per cent of couples still have less sex than before the pregnancy. Breastfeeding, however, does not seem to reduce the amount of sex couples have.

Survey data aren't that much help, because couples set their own levels of sexual activity and that's what they expect. They do, however, support the notion that men often want more sex than they're getting (does quality count for nothing?). A survey of over 800 adults by the health website Netdoctor found that nearly 80 per cent of men thought they weren't getting enough sex (compared with 60 per cent of women).

Babies and energetic children (are there any other kind?) reduce passion because they cause exhaustion. Your husband is clearly getting too much sleep if he's feeling passionate most nights of the week. Sex drives vary, and you don't say if your husband has always wanted more sex than you have wanted. But you need to negotiate with him not only how much sex you have but how much sleep he can help you to get.

STEP TO TAKE

My seventeen-year-old stepson takes my clothes and DVDs, comes in at 3 a.m. and sleeps until midday. He isn't at college, doesn't work and is rude and selfish. My girlfriend doesn't seem to do anything, although she knows I'm upset. We have a young daughter together and this isn't good for her. How can I get my girlfriend to see that her son is ruining our relationship?

It's hard being the stepfather to a teenage son. You may, however, have forgotten what you were like as a teenager – selfishness is part of the job description. It should pass. Teenagers can be tough for anyone to like, but research shows that step-parents find it harder to do so than biological parents. Step-parents have a difficult, undefined role; they often feel their parenting is undermined by the biological parent. Having their own children can make step-parents more intolerant of their stepchildren, as frequently they feel the contrast of the more fatherly or motherly feelings they have towards their own children. It's a common problem. Parentline Plus reckons that over 1 in 10 families are stepfamilies, with a total of 2 million children. In America the US Census Bureau says that over half of children aged thirteen and under live with a step-parent. In many countries (and in America already) the stepfamily will soon be the most common type of family.

Studies show that couples in stepfamilies struggle more than traditional families. A Joseph Rowntree study of 878 people bringing up children in stepfamilies found that both biological and step-parents had more relationship problems and argued more about how to bring up their children. Remarriages with stepchildren are more likely to split up than ones without. But enough about the grown-ups – it's harder for the stepchildren too. The Children's Society say that stepchildren are twice as likely as other kids to run away from home. It may be uncomfortable to acknowledge but there's considerable research showing that step-parents are less warm and supporting of stepchildren; put simply, less interested in them. This gets worse when they have their own children with their partner – largely because younger children need close monitoring. However, other studies are more optimistic, showing that relationships can grow closer over time, although adolescence is usually a low point.

Your girlfriend knows that you're upset and that her son's behaviour is unacceptable, but she has a loyalty to her son that you don't share. She may suspect you'd be more accommodating if your own daughter was behaving this way, whatever you say. She may also question whether you were sufficiently interested in him earlier to make it alright for you to be so angry now. You can't ignore that. But if you argue over his behaviour this will make your stepson's behaviour worse.

His behaviour alone is not ruining your relationship: it's also how you're dealing with it. You need to negotiate a united front and set your stepson boundaries that you both enforce. It's not good for him to live nocturnally and have no structure to his life. He may be a selfish seventeen-year-old but he may not be a very happy one. If his father has a good relationship with him, get him involved. Some families set up behavioural contracts with their teenagers that include rewards as well as sanctions, and you can get some help with organizations that work with families to develop these. These contracts can help set boundaries and ensure that as a family you keep talking to each other. You should try to develop some relationship with your stepson, even as you hunt for your favourite tee-shirt on his filthy floor. If it's any comfort, some middle-aged men might even be flattered that a teenager wants to wear their clothes.

FOR THE KIDS

I have been unhappy with my husband for years, and our marriage is effectively over. We don't row much but there's no affection or attraction between us, but he's a good dad and the children would be devastated if we divorced. Is it better to wait until the children leave home before we split up?

Deciding to divorce is not a trivial decision, but neither is staying in an unhappy marriage for the sake of the children. A report from the National Marriage Project in the United States cites a national survey fourteen years ago that found only 15 per cent of people agreed with the statement 'when there are children in the family, parents should stay together even if they don't get along'. The bar for not getting along has been lowered over the years.

But if you are going to put your children's happiness above your own, you'd want to know that staying together is measurably better for them. Particularly when no one else

seems to be doing it. In the UK figures from the Office for
National Statistics show that 10 per cent of all families are
stepfamilies and almost 1 in 4 children lives in a single-parent
family. In the United States, a paper in the journal *Social
Work* in 2003 estimated that one third of people are part
of a stepfamily. There is a huge research literature on the
effects of divorce on children, and although some children
do fantastically well afterwards, the pointers are mostly in the
opposite direction.

One study on delaying divorce, from the University of
Pennsylvania and the London School of Economics, uses
data from 11,407 people who took part in the National Child
Development Study. The people in the study were thirty-
three years old and divided into whether they were children
(seven to sixteen) or older when their parents divorced. Those
whose parents had divorced when they were children did
less well educationally and were more likely to be poor and
have children early in life. But the researchers argue that all
studies overstate the effects of divorce because they fail to take
into account how the children were brought up in the family
before the divorce.

There isn't strong evidence that delaying divorce prevents
serious fallout, although the overall effects of divorce include,
according to a report from the Vanier Institute of the Family,
an increased risk of poverty, depression, doing poorly at
school, becoming a young offender, teenage pregnancy and
relationship problems. The report does say, however, that
the average differences in these misfortunes in children
of divorced versus those from intact families is not huge.
On a more mundane level, children miss the other parent.
Sometimes terribly. The Vanier Institute report also says
that although divorces which end parental conflict can have
positive effects for children, in those families where parents

have got on fairly well, a divorce can be shocking for the children because they never expected it.

Two parents are generally thought to be better than one if they support each other in bringing up their children. Divorce, it should be noted, is sufficiently stressful to make it hard to be a parent, at least for a while. If you are motivated enough to stay in this marriage for the children, is it so impossible to try to improve it for yourself? Talking to your husband, getting outside help (but you have to want to try) and seeing if you can salvage it would be better for all of you.

Testing Times

FIRST FEELINGS

Out of the blue I've had an email from my first real
girlfriend. We split up when I went to college. She says she's
happily married and just wanted to say hi, but I was quite
shocked. I'm married with two children and I'm not sure I
should reply. Should I just press delete?

Yes, if you want to preserve the relationship you've already
got. Early loves are incredibly powerful, and with the internet
increasingly accessible. A survey in *Time* magazine in 2000
found that out of over 3,000 people nearly 60 per cent said
they often thought about their first loves. Dr Nancy Kalish
from California State University has done the bulk of research
into what she calls 'lost loves' following her own experience
(which did not work out). In her 2004 survey of 1,300
randomly selected adults from all over America one third said
they would reunite with their first loves if they could. She
estimates that 10 per cent of people try to get in touch with
a lost love. There are no numbers for those who get in touch

and within minutes remember exactly why they split up in the first place.

By advertising in the media, Kalish has data on 2,500 couples who reunited. Most (around 84 per cent) reunited with someone they'd loved before the age of twenty-two. Usually they'd split up because they'd been too young, moved away, or their parents had disapproved. The reasons were external, usually out of their control and nothing to do with how well they got on, and many of the couples felt angry about it for years. People who split up because they were cheated on, unhappy or bored do not seem to go back for more.

The first 1,000 couples Kalish found in the 1990s were mostly single when they found their lost loves. Once they met, things moved quickly, with 40 per cent of them together within three weeks. Most then married, with over 70 per cent still together in 2004 (these figures may be skewed, because Kalish included everyone in her counting – even those married for a few months). Couples said they felt emotionally intense and comfortable with each other. But the familiarity did not make things dull. Sexually, these couples felt more like they were slipping into red stilettos than beige slippers.

Why are these relationships so compelling? Psychiatrists from the University of California talk of early love experiences being chemically hardwired into the brain. Your ex grew up with you, knows your family and most likely set the standard for love. You shared friends, hopes and cult television programmes. There's a lot to talk about. These were not insignificant relationships at the time. Kalish found that many of the first loves she found had been together initially for two to five years and had mourned the relationship for anything up to three years.

But before you pull up that email again, Kalish's more recent couples, who are rather different to the earlier group that she researched, are not happy. Most have casually googled in a speculative fashion, with no plan for what to do if they found their lost love. They were mostly already in committed, usually happy, relationships and 80 per cent ended up having affairs with their lost loves. Kalish hasn't finished analysing the data but believes only a small proportion look like making it long-term. The destruction it causes families makes her almost evangelical in telling people not to press reply. Unless you are single. And you aren't.

FATAL ATTRACTION

I was attracted to my boyfriend because he was gorgeous and easy-going. I have a high-powered job and liked his lack of ambition. But now it's driving me mad and I'm embarrassed when he tells friends he works in a charity shop and watches daytime TV. Is it perverse of me to want to split up from him because of this? It's why I used to like him.

Gorgeous is always attractive and may explain any oversight in other areas. I don't know how long you've been together, but lust and both being on your best behaviour means it can take an age to assess long-term potential.

Falling for qualities you later detest is termed by sociologist Diane Femlee, who researched this phenomenon at the

University of California at Davis, 'fatal attraction'. She
lifted the name from the film, in which (for those who have
never seen it) an initially sexy and wild woman becomes a
crazy bunny boiler (where that term comes from, in fact).
In research published in *Personal Relationships*, Femlee asked
over 301 men and women (students at an American West
Coast university) to recall the last serious relationship they'd
had that had broken up. What specific qualities, she asked,
attracted you, and which ones, she asked further down her
questionnaire, did you find least attractive? A third cited looks,
1 in 5 a sense of humour and 12 per cent said intelligence.
Only 2 per cent of people rated being easy-going, so you're
in a minority there. But many qualities in retrospect had a
downside (although you may want to take these results with
a pinch of sour grapes because these were ex's). The qualities
most likely to be adored and later loathed were 'exciting',
'different' and, guess what, 'easy-going'. 'Confidence' became
'arrogance', 'funny' turned into 'immature' and 'spontaneous'
became 'weird'. Even characteristics that you'd think everyone
would love, like 'caring', became twisted into 'possessive'.
The more people raved about a quality, the more likely it was
later to end up on the things-I-hate-most list. When someone
called a quality unique, this characteristic was three times
more likely than others to be one of the reasons for ending the
relationship.

One third of people reported breaking up with someone
because of a quality that they no longer found attractive. In
particular it was the differences between couples (he's so
easy-going and I am so ambitious) that are initially attractive
that become more noticeable and annoying once that first
attraction is over. Also, studies show that the length of
relationships is related to the support they get from friends
and family. If your friends are all high-fliers, they may subtly

or blatantly undermine your relationship. They may never be able to see what you saw in him.

Only you know if you want someone more ambitious. At least start talking to him about how you feel. Not in a critical way but as a genuine attempt to see if this disenchantment is real. Relationships do fluctuate, especially in the early days. You may be surprised. He may think you want him to be home when you come in, and you may find he really craves a job in banking. Femlee's study found one woman who complained her ex had been too sweet and sensitive. She found out how wrong she was when he went out with her best friend.

FINGERS TO THE BONE

My partner doesn't appreciate how much housework and running around after the kids I do. We both work full time and my job is as busy as his. How can I get him to stop taking what I do at home for granted?

There's an old-fashioned saying that goes, 'I like hugs, I like kisses, but what I love is help with the dishes' – and sadly it still has a certain resonance. A Pew Research Center survey in 2007 of 2,000 Americans found that sharing household chores was given as the third most popular factor for a happy marriage. It came ahead of money, a nice house and even having children. A total of 62 per cent said it was important, compared to only 7 per cent who thought it didn't matter.

Sharing household chores is now nipping at the heels of the second most highly rated factor – a good sex life. Faithfulness was number one. And if you're a woman, the amount of sex you have and the amount of housework your partner does may not be unrelated. Some women find 'chore-play', as it's called when men do housework, makes them more sexually interested in their partner. Not because dusting is erotic but because sharing household tasks makes for fairer relationships and intimacy, which is erotic. No wonder that a coffee-table book called *Porn for Women*, which has hunky men, fully dressed, in aprons, doing housework, has done so well.

The amount of housework that men do has been rising steadily. The Council on Contemporary Families in America says that a study from twenty industrialized countries covering 1965 to 2003 shows men's contribution to family work rose from less than one fifth in 1965 to more than a third by 2003. The latest Time Use Survey in the UK carried out by the Office for National Statistics shows that women do two thirds of housework – 178 minutes a day compared with 100 minutes by men (who did more of the DIY repairs and gardening, which were also counted as housework). Women who work full time still do more housework – 42 per cent clean and tidy, compared with 17 per cent of men.

So what happens in lesbian couples, particularly if they have children, which is when most friction around sharing housework occurs? A small study of twenty-nine lesbian couples in the *Journal of Social and Personal Relationships* found that after couples had children women still shared their housework quite equally – but the biological mother spent more time on childcare. Generally studies show men spend more time with their children than ever before, but so do women.

So if housework is viewed as optional for men (especially your man), it's up to you to change things. You need to discuss what you think needs doing and what each of you will do. If you have different thresholds for what is dirty and what needs cleaning, then you will have to negotiate. You will also need to give him credit for his DIY. If you continue to feel hard done by, it will threaten your relationship. But if things get better don't be tempted to get married. Generally, men who live with someone do more housework than if they got married.

NAG OR NEGOTIATE?

I feel as if I'm nagging my partner all the time. I am forever saying, 'Will you put the bin out?' or 'Do you think you could make lunch for the kids for a change?' I'm sure he thinks I'm a nag, and it doesn't work as he 'forgets'. How can I get him to do things without nagging?

Nagging doesn't work, as you've discovered, and what's more it's rather unattractive. Nagging, for those who don't do it, is asking someone to do something repeatedly in many different ways, sometimes using different voices (that sound increasingly exasperated). By virtue of having to ask over and over again, nagging is not effective and makes the recipient angry and defensive. This is not to say that the request you originally made is not valid. But relationship experts suggest saying five positive things to your partner for every one negative thing in order to nurture a satisfying relationship, and nagging makes this rather difficult.

It's usually women who are accused of nagging, not men. So is this fair? A study in the *Journal of Pragmatics* from the University of Florida asked students to collect examples of nagging during Thanksgiving – a family occasion for which nagging was invented. Out of seventy examples of nagging, women were reported to have done the nagging in two thirds, and it was mostly over their partner doing (or not doing) a wide range of housework tasks. In the remaining third of the nagging examples (done by men), there were only six examples of the types of things men nagged about, mostly non-domestic issues such as slamming the car door. The researchers suggested that women might have more to nag about.

Nagging is an example of what psychologists call 'demand-withdraw behaviour'. When something matters to only one person, the other one ignores it. How this works is shown in a study of fifty married couples in the *Journal of Marriage and Family*. Researchers videoed the couples' discussions of the five most important changes their spouse could make in their behaviour that would improve their relationship. The more spouses had to lose by changing their behaviour, the more they withdrew from the discussion. And this led to nagging. Put simply, your partner ignores requests to put out the bin because he can't be bothered to get up and carry a smelly bin down the path. Did you know that already?

No one would suggest this is good behaviour, but it may be easier to work round it. A study in the *Journal of Experimental Social Psychology* by a professor who wanted to understand why her husband did the opposite of what she wanted him to do showed that people often do so unconsciously. It is human nature for some people to avoid doing what someone else wants them to do, in order to retain their autonomy. Confronting a psychological imperative head on may be frustrating for both of you.

You could try to re-phrase your requests or focus on the bigger issue of negotiating how you share household chores. Stay calm and discuss the nagging. Communicate clearly how you feel about how much you both do around the house. It should work better if you can phrase your discussion in a positive way, for example, 'I would really appreciate it if you could put the bin out as it's the one thing I hate doing.' Avoid being accusatory and getting cross. If you hear yourself saying, 'You never think of doing' – well, just about anything really – then the discussion is going badly. If nothing works, you may have more fundamental problems. Let's hope you don't – they certainly won't be solved by nagging.

WHO MOANS MOST?

I've just come back from a weekend with my girlfriends, and those of us with relationships spent a lot of time talking about the problems we have with our men. I know that my boyfriend's mates on their boys' weekend away didn't spend time talking about their relationships. Do women moan more about their relationships than men and if so why?

Of course women moan more about their relationships to their friends than men do. The research shows that women not only complain of more problems but also feel lonelier when they're in relationships (they're programmed for intimacy) and are more likely to leave. Figures from the Office for National Statistics in the UK show that two thirds of divorces are initiated by women, most of whom cite their husband's unreasonable behaviour, a category that could include failing to meet expectations. Men, on the other hand, divorce most often on the more unimaginative or less judgemental grounds that they've been separated for two years. Generally, men seem to be easier to please.

To moan so much, women must have clear ideas of what they want in relationships and thus be able to pinpoint exactly when and how their men fall short of expectations. But do women want from their relationships things that are different from what men want? A study in the journal *Personal Relationships* asked 122 people who had been in relationships for an average of eleven years (they were aged between twenty-three and fifty-nine) to rate the importance of thirty standards for relationships. The standards were obvious stuff: that they and their partner showed they liked each other, talked to each other (about feelings not just the electricity bill) and were faithful. The study found that men and women agreed on the relative importance of each standard, but that women felt their standards were met less often than men did. Since a lot of the standards were about communication and intimacy, traditionally female strengths, women were bound to do better in them.

Even when men did feel their standards weren't being met they were less bothered by it than women were. Women are just more aware of how their relationships are doing. There are other studies that show that women monitor more closely than men how their relationships are going. They are therefore more likely than men to notice if the relationship falls short and can feel aggrieved by it.

Psychologists would argue that women aren't moaning about their relationships: they are 'working on them' (and these are psychologists of both sexes). Men (in psychology studies at least) will say their friendships are 'activity' based: they talk more to other men about the form of their football team than the form their relationships are in. Women are more likely to confide in their close friends about practically everything, in detail that may be finer than their men would like. There's good evidence that when women talk about their relationships, they feel supported by doing so. This may be because such conversations help them talk through the problems they have with their partners or because friendships provide the intimacy 'top-up' missing from their relationship. Friends may support the relationship rather then denigrate it, particularly if they like the partner. But of course the real reason why women moan about their relationships is that there's nothing to say about them (and none of their friends would be interested) when they're going well.

TOO MANY TODDIES?

My husband and I are in our late sixties and have a good marriage. However, my husband is drinking more. He'll have a bottle of wine on the go before midday and drink two to three bottles a day (hiding his glass), but if I mention it he says, 'So what, I'm not working any more.' Our relationship has deteriorated – drinking makes him argumentative. He says it isn't a problem, but I think it is. What can I do?

It seems that quite a few older people are drinking more than is good for them. Psychiatrists have coined the term 'Saga louts' for men like your husband, who spend their retirement catching up on their alcohol consumption rather than on more socially useful activities. They are a rather hidden phenomenon, however, as instead of throwing up in the city centre on a Saturday night they drink excessively in the privacy of their own homes. A community-based study in the *International Journal of Addiction* found that around 2 to 4 per cent of older people were in the alcoholic bracket, while data from the General Household Survey put 17 per cent of men and 7 per cent of women in the drinking excessively category.

A 2006 article in the *British Journal of Psychiatry* says that older people are one of the groups least informed about alcohol units, and this may be part of the problem. And should anyone be able to remember them, the recommended drinking levels may not be as applicable for older people because age and some medications reduce the ability to metabolize alcohol. However, the American advice of one drink a day for older people, while clear cut, is thought by many European doctors to be so restrictive as to be draconian.

Alcohol makes people defensive (as well as offensive), so your husband is unlikely to admit to drinking too much. (And people who drink too much don't usually admit it, because they associate an alcohol problem with homeless drunks swigging meths, not with respectable folk like themselves sipping good wine.) How much is too much is hard to define unless you're following the recommended maximum units (currently over twenty-one for men and fourteen for women a week), but if you feel he is drinking too much then you're probably right. But perhaps most important, do you have any idea why your husband is drinking more? Is it just because he can, or does he, in retirement, feel depressed or lonely? Retirement takes some adjustment. There may have been another stressful event that has triggered his drinking problem.

Research into relationships where one partner drinks heavily shows they're unhappy and fraught with arguments, usually about how much the partner's drinking. There's always the risk that fights can get violent. GPs are more aware of this these days and some offer brief interventions that aim to reduce the amount people drink; these involve a few educational sessions about safe limits and the use of alcohol diaries (to document intake rather than to record drunken moments). Older people can usually be helped to drink within the limits again. But often for a brief intervention to be taken up the person has to have some insight into the fact that they have a problem – they may have fallen over when drunk or been caught driving when over the limit. There is also the Alcoholics Anonymous option. AA has a sister fellowship called AL-Anon for people like yourself whose life is affected by others' drinking. You may want to start with this, as your husband is unlikely to skip into an AA meeting if he is in denial. You should tell him you are going because you are worried about his drinking and suggest he gets some help himself. What isn't an option is to spend your retirement with a partner who's permanently pissed.

'WE' TIME

My boyfriend and I have busy jobs, and although we live together we rarely spend any proper time in each other's company. He says it doesn't matter, it's just a phase, our work is demanding and it will pass. I don't think other couples live like that. How much time do most people spend together, and does it matter?

Couples spend much less time together than you'd think. The Office for National Statistics does regular time-use surveys – the sort that also finds you spend two years of your life cutting your toe-nails. These show that our time is mostly divided between sleep, work and watching television. On average we spend two to two and a half hours a day with our partners, including weekends. Add in children, and just over one of those hours disappears into playing schools or re-arranging plastic dinosaurs. And what do we do when we're alone with our loved ones? Watch television (one third of all the time spent together), eat (30 minutes) and do housework together (24 minutes). Whoopee. Married people spend half-an-hour more together than people who cohabit. (The mystery is how retired couples spend only four hours a day together. Are they avoiding each other?)

For many, this lack of time with partners is a problem. An ICM poll of 2,004 adults in 2007 found that 64 per cent of men and women cited spending time with their family or finding time for their key relationships as their biggest concern – ahead of money and health. So clearly it worries many people, if not your partner.

By asking your partner for 'proper time' you presumably mean time when you interact. Television can be passive unless you have a lively chat about the programmes you've seen. A study from the Brigham Young University and Colorado State University tracked the leisure activity and relationship of 318 couples who were married or lived together. They found that women cared more than men about spending time together but were clear that the time had to involve talking to each other. If you can't remember what an activity like that would be, think of visiting a place of interest (an art gallery rather than a pub) or cooking together. Whatever you do together as a couple you need to talk to each other either during or after it to make it a communal activity. Just being with your partner doesn't make your relationship better.

So of course it matters if you don't spend much time together or if that time is spent having a TV dinner, or working on adjacent lap-tops. A study in the *Journal of Sex Research* of 6,029 couples from the US National Survey of Families and Households found (somewhat obviously) that the less time couples spent together, the less sex they had. It's worse if you or your partner feels overwhelmed by work. A study from Penn State University studied the quality of the relationships that 190 men had with their wives and their teenage children. It found that there's a world of difference in how happy couples are when they've agreed on the longer hours (perhaps to afford to move house) compared to when they hadn't.

Don't just hope that things will get better. Phases have a tendency to develop into the natural order of things. Suggest that you spend a least one evening a week together, either at home but talking to each other or on a 'date'. The Office for National Statistics' survey suggests that if you don't make time for each other, you'll have a whole relationship, not just a phase, that's based on sleeping and television.

INCOME-LINKED DIVORCE

*My wife earns more than I do. This was true when I met
her and it's never bothered me. Since we've had children
I do more childcare and housework than she does. I read
somewhere that couples where wives are the higher earners
have a 50 per cent higher divorce rate than couples in which
the husband earns more. Is this true?*

The number of women working and the amount they earn
has gone up (although men still earn on average 12.6 per cent
more according to the Office for National Statistics), as has
the divorce rate. But this is not cause and effect.

Women who are the main breadwinners are still a minority.
Most women in this category are not high-flying bankers
but low earners whose partners earn less or are unemployed.
Research from America (there don't seem to be equivalent
UK studies) is not conclusive. One study showed that for
every $5,000 increase in wives' income, the odds of divorce
increased by 5 per cent. Other studies show that wives'
earnings reduce the risk of divorce by making the couples'
lives more comfortable and making them have more to lose
financially by splitting up. A paper by the Family Policy
Studies Centre in the UK says that most families need two
incomes to maintain a reasonable standard of living and
that couples negotiate the amount of time they each work as
their circumstances, including their relative contributions to
income, change.

The old-fashioned concerns around a wife earning more than her husband are that it's unnatural and will turn him into a resentful, inadequate girl's blouse and that a wife who earns more will leave at the slightest excuse because she can afford to. Economic dependency has traditionally been thought to make women more committed to their marriages. However, attitudes have changed. A survey by the dating website True.com, which has 2.7 million users, found that a third of their male users (no numbers given) actually wanted women who earned more than they did.

Most of the studies citing higher divorce rates are old and flawed, because they used individuals instead of couples and so couldn't find out if divorces were due to one person holding traditional views about a man's income and status, or the fact that the wife brought home the larger slice of bacon. How much importance men and women attach to work is clearly significant. One of the more thorough studies, of a randomized group of 286 dual-earning couples, published in the *Journal of Marriage and Family*, found that only men who felt defined by their salary became upset if their wives earned more. Which is still a lot of men. The study showed that women didn't mind earning more, and since they don't have the historical baggage of linking self-worth to salary they don't care if they earn less either. What made them happy in relationships were husbands, like you, who did their share of childcare and housework.

Another study, using the National Survey of Families and Households, which includes over 5,000 American couples, found that both men and women were happier when the husband was the major breadwinner (and this study is only a few years old). But the single most important factor in deciding how happy a woman was in her marriage was nothing to do with income. Above all, they wanted men who were emotionally involved. The latter being something that money can't buy.

OUTLAW THE IN-LAWS?

My mother-in-law is critical of me and makes snide comments. My husband doesn't seem to notice but gets upset if I get upset. Since we have had our son, who is two, it has got worse and she comes round more. We got on better before the marriage. Should I ban her from the house, have it out with her, or rise above it?

These are all fair options if your mother-in law is criticizing you. Unfortunately, while there's research on strife with the mother-in-law (and tons of feeble jokes), there aren't any studies on what to do about it. There are websites such as the Secret Society of Tortured Daughters-in-Law (www. tortureddaughtersinlaw.com) and one that advertises help for Parents-in-Law Phobia (changethatsrightnow.com) and offers a therapy programme. Essentially they'd probably support (husband willing) a ban.

You both love the same man, and that doesn't usually work. You understand mother love yourself now – how fierce and unconditional it is. Imagine your son grown up with a girlfriend or wife and how you would watch and possibly judge her. This isn't to excuse your mother-in-law's behaviour, but it's worth understanding it. How sure can you be that when you're a mother-in-law you'll do any better?

As you begin bringing up your young family, your mother-in-law has finished that phase of her life. Ideally, she should maintain a limited interest in yours and be involved when you ask her rather than as she sees fit. But your negative relationship with her will infect your marriage. A study of the influence of in-laws on the success of marriages by Iowa State University found that couples in which the wife and mother-in-law didn't get on were more likely to split up than those in which there wasn't conflict. Out of the 403 husbands they studied, thirty-three got divorced over four years, and conflict between wives and mothers-in-law had a significantly negative effect on the marriages. Other studies show that once a couple has children this is often a source of tension with mothers-in-law, who feel they know best about all aspects of child rearing.

A team from the University of Arkansas interviewed twenty-three daughters-in-law and nineteen mothers-in-law. It found that tensions arose from the slightest things. Wives didn't like their mothers-in-law leaving phone messages only for their husband. Mothers-in-law felt hurt when their daughters-in-law didn't rush to greet them at social events. The relationship often deteriorated over wedding plans and imagined slights.

Mothers-in-law are less judgmental about their daughters-in-law than vice versa (all the studies show this) and are often mystified as to how they have offended them. Getting to know your mother-in-law as a woman in her own right outside of polite family gatherings may make it easier for both of you to tolerate each other. So, before you ban her, get to know her a bit better.

Be kind to her and have a talk with your husband about how she makes you feel. Remember not to call her anything that will upset him, because that witch is his mother. Ask him for ideas on how to deal with it and present a united front if you need to confront her criticisms. Fortunately, though, there is good research that suggests that too much contact with the in-laws causes trouble, so you shouldn't see too much of her – as if you didn't know that already.

PATHETIC PRESENTS

I love Christmas and I work hard to make it special for the family. But my partner's presents to me are so disappointing. He's lovely and we get on well, but his presents are so functional and unromantic that I feel hurt by them. One year he got me a mobile phone charger. I get upset that he either doesn't know me at all or doesn't care enough. Shall I tell him what to buy me – which takes the fun out of it?

Does telling your man what to buy you for Christmas take the fun out of it? Well, it's not much fun now, is it? The easiest option is to direct him to a survey such as one from Pricegrabber.com, which has 21 million users a month, showing that the top gifts women want are jewellery and clothing. Mobile phone chargers don't feature; neither do foot spas or cordless irons. An overwhelming 1 per cent of women said they wanted a DIY product. Men (in case you're interested) want the latest electrical gizmo, often a television. They are also more likely to assume that women, like them, want something useful.

Most surveys show that women put more effort into and spend more money at Christmas. Dr Anne Wilson, a social psychologist at Wilfrid Laurier University in Canada says that women more than men think of gifts as communicating emotional purpose. Men will be happy with a DIY gadget because ... hey, tools are useful. But does your partner's present mean he doesn't know you? Wilson says that too often we make assumptions that our partners know us better than they actually do. The notion that people close to you can read you like an open book is just wrong, particularly at Christmas.

You suggest his useless present-buying has even deeper meaning – that it reflects how (little) he feels about you. This is unlikely to be true and is rather unfair on him. In fact, your response says more about you than his gift. Research shows that women spend more time than men judging how responsive their partner is. Men assume (forgive the generalizations) that if they're happy then so is their partner. In a study led by Dr Sandra Murray from the University of Buffalo, 173 couples kept a daily diary of how they got on (measured by psychological scoring systems). Lots of them felt occasionally hurt by their partner, but those who felt confident about themselves responded by trying to get closer to their partner. Those who didn't behaved in ways guaranteed to push their partner away by being distant or moody. Most of the people who felt undervalued underestimated how much their partners cared about them and how happy their partners were in the relationship. In fact, the people who agonized over why their partners stayed with them were loved just as much as others who felt more secure. So check your self-esteem, tell him exactly what you want for Christmas and, in the interests of getting closer, go and buy him the latest TV. If you can't afford that, try a nice drill instead.

QUESTION OF MISERY

I had a miscarriage two months ago. I was only about six weeks pregnant and have two small children, and although I felt sad, I was almost relieved. However, my partner still seems upset, and we are now quite distant from each other. Is this normal, and will it get better? I feel a bit cross that he's miserable when I'm the one who had the miscarriage.

You alone had the miscarriage but you'd both have had the baby. Around 1 in 4 pregnancies end in miscarriage, and even when they occur early on they are unsettling and distressing, however ambivalent you feel about the pregnancy. And like many difficulties in relationships it's as likely to pull you apart as push you together. A study in the *Journal of Perinatology* shows that 85 per cent of couples share their feelings about miscarriage in a limited way, if at all. Men worry so much about saying the wrong thing that, guess what, they may say nothing at all.

Traditionally there's been less attention paid to the reaction of men after miscarriages because the physical effects of a miscarriage belong so exclusively to the woman. But a study in the journal *Evolutionary Psychology* that asked over 300 men in the north of England how they felt after their partner's miscarriage found that while men were less acutely distressed, they had more difficulty coping long-term. Some of the men reported feeling grief and despair. Men will have felt the baby to be less real than their partner during the pregnancy but still feel the loss at the miscarriage – especially if they have seen the baby on an ultrasound scan. The men in the study also said they were worried about their partner's health and feelings. Other studies show that men can feel a range of emotions (including nothing) such as empathy, powerlessness, fear of the future and sometimes resentment about the whole business.

So this is why your partner feels upset. But why are you feeling cross? Feeling angry after a miscarriage is common, as is depression and anxiety. When we feel sad it's normal, if unattractive, to take it out on those dearest to us. But maybe you feel your partner is so busy being sad that he isn't supporting you. A study of 185 women led by Kristen Swanson, a professor of family and child nursing, and researchers from the University of Washington found that one year after miscarriage, one third of couples were more distant, avoiding sex and feeling tense with each other. This was more likely to happen when women couldn't discuss their loss with their partner and felt unloved and unsupported. Women are more likely to feel depressed and angry if their partner won't talk about the miscarriage and better able to cope when their partners shows they care – preferably by making a fuss of them.

It's normal for you to have reacted differently. Women feel better about miscarriages when they share their feelings; men often feel they are treading on eggshells when they do so. What you must do is be kind and patient to each other and talk about what's happened, accepting you won't feel the same. It will be worth it. The Washington study found that the other two thirds of couples said their relationships after miscarriage were either as good as they had been before or even closer and happier.

HAVING YOUR CAKE

I've been in a relationship for six years but recently met this man when our children played together in the park. He's a single parent, and we've met a few times with the children and once on our own. I'm completely blown away by him. I think I'm in love and want to be with him, but I really love my boyfriend. Can you be in love with two people at the same time?

You might think there's no research to answer your question (which is as much philosophical as psychological), and you'd be right. How can you know if you're in love with him? An online survey of over 1,100 readers of *Psychology Today* (many of whom are psychologists) found that two thirds thought you could be in love with more than one person at once. Support comes from parental love (which embraces more than one child), and if you don't buy that because it's asexual, there are some polygamous love marriages (and polygamy has strict rules to avoid favouritism). Most people have friends who feel that they have been in love with two people at once. Should anything come of it, this can also be known as infidelity, which sounds far less lofty.

Psychologists have tried to measure styles of loving using such devices as the Love Attitude Scale. At the heart of these, aside from passion and intensity, are the attributes of friendship, dependency, altruism and commitment. Is it possible to be altruistic and committed to two men? Is it possible to feel that much for someone you don't know that well? The Passionate Love Scale – where love is defined as an intense longing to be with someone – asks how preoccupied you are when thinking about them, how much you want to please and be with them. It has equal amounts of pain and pleasure. But any scale has only limited value – for researchers rather than individuals. No scales can package love as a block of measurable science – there's emotion and compulsion in love.

Another type of measurable love, companionate love, is defined by psychologists as the more committed type of love, based on having lives that are strongly intertwined. Ideally, relationships have both. What often happens is that companionate love loses enough of its passion to make other people, who have that edginess of attraction, more appealing.

One important point is that psychologists say that you're unlikely to be in love with two people at the same time who are similar. Your boyfriend may be pragmatic, your new love a poet. Some also say (brace yourself) that healthy people are satisfied in a relationship with one person and only narcissists and people with dysfunctional emotional lives think they can be in love with two people at the same time. Sorry about that.

Your existing relationship is likely to win out because there's more invested in it, unless you proceed to have an affair, which will seriously damage your existing relationship. Stop seeing this new man and improve the relationship with your old one. Breathe back into it some of the life that may been extinguished by children and familiarity. Some people may advise you to go for this new love (although it seems speculative to call it love just yet) because your happiness is the most important thing. But that would be tough on your and his children and also on your boyfriend. It's analogous to driving a comfortable, steady Ford and seeing a shiny Porsche that makes your heart race again. Choosing a newer model may or may not be the right choice, but it would certainly be the most costly for everyone concerned.

Happily Ever After

NOT JUST A FILM

We've been married for seven years this October. We have a daughter who's three, and we get on pretty well compared to other couples we know. But I wonder if there's really such a thing as a seven-year itch, and if so what can you do to prevent it?

The idea of a seven-year itch comes from the film of that name starring Marilyn Monroe, who looked rather tempting when her dress was blown upwards by a subway vent. In real life, the Office for National Statistics says that 19 per cent of divorces happen between nought and four years, 27 per cent between five and nine years, and 13 per cent between fifteen and nineteen years. The median length of marriage in England is now around seven years for women marrying between the ages of twenty-five and thirty-four. In America, according to Larry Bumpass, professor at the University of Wisconsin, one half of marriages ends before seven years. Couples who live together start scratching earlier: John Ermisch from the

University of Essex says that for women in their thirties the median time they live with a partner is three and a half years.

The seven-year itch reflects couples' disillusionment with each other more than a search for alternatives (over 50 per cent of women cite unreasonable behaviour as a reason for divorce, as do 31 per cent of men). Generally, the honeymoon period is over quickly. It used to be cute that he ate cold beans from a tin, now it's disgusting. There's a deafening sound of scales falling from eyes within the first four years. Many studies have looked at this potentially depressing phenomenon, one such being carried out over a period of eight years by Lawrence Kurdek and published in *Developmental Psychology*. He compared the answers from 538 couples (one of the problems is that only 93 couples were left by the end of the study – and maybe they were the unhappiest) to over thirty questions, such as how affectionate and dependable their partners were and how much they agreed on important issues. He also asked about 'dysfunctional beliefs', so listen up, as they include thinking that arguing is bad (it's how you argue that counts), that sex should be perfect and that your partner should intuitively understand you. He found a clear dip in happiness after four years and another around eight years when the couples were questioned again, particularly for couples with children and those previously divorced. Not surprisingly, he advises couples to modify their expectations. Prepare, in fact, for disappointment, because it is likely to happen.

Research by John M. Gottman, one of America's best-known relationship researchers, shows that it's possible to predict with 94 per cent accuracy which couples will divorce, even before they marry, after watching them talk for a few minutes on a thorny issue. Couples that say five positive things to one negative are likely to survive. Below that they're in trouble. Gottman has also studied gay and lesbian couples, and in a study published in the *Journal of Homosexuality* he reported that these couples are less belligerent, fairer and more considerate to each other. They were generally better at resolving rows. In heterosexual relationships, if the man listens to the woman in a dispute (really, I'm not making this up), if they can avoid sneering at each other (contempt, says Gottman, is sulphuric acid for relationships), criticizing or withdrawing (what tactics are you left with then?), it may make for a rubbish argument, but it reduces the risk of scratching after seven years.

LEAVING THE NEST

My daughter goes to university this year. My son moved out two years ago. My husband and I will soon be on our own together. Although we get on pretty well, I dread it really. I've heard of couples splitting up after twenty years of marriage once their children have left home. What usually happens to couples when their children leave home?

The risk of empty-nest syndrome (depression and loss of purpose) after your children have left home has been rather exaggerated. Mothers used to be prescribed antidepressants by their family doctor before their children had shut the door behind them. But most mothers are actually happier once their children move out. That psychological umbilical cord may be strong, but a mother's (and father's) job is to cut it and launch their children into independent adult lives. That your kids will never be able to afford a mortgage unless you can stump up the deposit is a small detail.

Mothers undoubtedly do miss their children, but they get over it. A study of 318 mothers by the Battelle Human Affairs Research Center in Seattle measured their psychological well-being before and after their youngest child had left home. It found that after six months to a year (well, you'll miss them initially) most women felt much happier once their children had moved out. They were only upset if their children were not coping in the outside world. A similar and more recent study from the University of Melbourne of 438 women also found that mothers reported fewer daily hassles and that they felt better when their children left home – but only if they weren't worrying about them.

So do happy mothers mean happier marriages? (The research is not clear on how fathers feel, but traditionally they are thought to be less upset.) Some experts, such as Dr Karen Fingerman, Associate Professor of Developmental and Family Studies at the University of Michigan, have said that most parents enjoy 'reconnecting' with their spouses and also get on better with their children once they've left home. They also, if they put their minds to it, have a great time. A survey of 1,190 parents by the insurance firm Zurich shows that 42 per cent of empty-nesters take more holidays together and 36 per cent spend more quality time (including having sex again) with their partner. Are you still dreading it?

With the children gone there is the fear that your relationship will be exposed as past its sell-by date – that you'll have nothing left to talk about. The research is inconclusive on whether empty-nesters are more likely to divorce. Some couples do delay leaving unhappy marriages until their children grow up, and the baby boomer generation have form for the pursuit of individual happiness; but there is some research that shows marriages grow stronger as the stress of having children around disappears, and longer marriages are also stronger because they have more invested in them. That said, one US study did find that for couples married twenty years, an empty nest increased their chances of divorce, but for those married twenty-eight years or more it reduced it. Doing things together and talking (nicely) to each other improves your chances of staying together. So you should enjoy yourselves and start spending your children's inheritance before they finish university and move back in again.

REDUNDANCY RECOVERY

My partner was made redundant five months ago. My job means we're okay financially, and he is trying to find work, but he's moody – there's no affection or sex. If it carries on he'll lose me as well as his job. How much of this is inevitable with redundancy? Can I make things better?

It's not hard to imagine what it feels like to lose your job, income, structure to your day and the answer to 'What do you do?' The reality is probably ten times as bad. So your partner is moody? Lost his libido? Perfectly normal. Be thankful he's not suffered anything worse. A study in the *British Medical Journal* of 6,191 men aged between forty and fifty-nine found that those who lost their jobs during the five years of the study were twice as likely to die as those who didn't. When social class, smoking, drinking and existing health problems were taken into account the risk of dying fell, but only slightly. These men had been in steady employment for the five years before the study and so were normal healthy working folk. However, relax: this isn't to say redundancy kills you – it's only an association. What redundancy does do for many people is take away their reason for getting up in the morning.

Other studies show that redundancy causes depression (not an unsurprising finding) and a tendency to drink more alcohol than is good for you. There is some evidence that it can increase the risk of suicide. But it partly depends on the circumstances of the redundancy. If it happens through a massive downsizing or when unemployment is high it's less damaging to couples because it doesn't reflect on the person being made redundant. It's nothing to do with them – it's the economy, stupid. There is some evidence that redundancy makes marriages more precarious. A study by the Institute of Social and Economic Research using a large Swedish data set found that a job loss increased the risk of divorce by 18 per cent in the first year. This was true whether it was men or women who lost their jobs. The author speculates that it's not the job loss itself or financial issues (he cites generous welfare benefits in Sweden) but something more subtle that erodes relationships. Such as the redundant person feeling that their partner can't understand and will find them less attractive.

Couples who can cope financially and get support from friends and family are more likely to stay together after a redundancy. So get some help. Enlist his friends to take him out. Talk to him kindly. Say you want to be with him but he seems unhappy and distant. Could he reconsider this approach to his redundancy? Be affectionate and make it clear you find him attractive. Encourage him to use his time to sort things out in the house (every house needs some sorting out) and reassure him that he is more likely than not to find another job, but it may take some time. Tell him that while you understand how tough this is and how much he is struggling, you miss the old him. To you, the job he used to have was never the most important thing about him.

SOFA SO GOOD?

My partner says we need to have counselling for our relationship. I agree with her that we've grown apart: we argue a lot and rarely have sex or spend any quality time together. I'm committed to this relationship (we have two children), but can counselling save our relationship or has she already made up her mind to leave?

Relationship counselling can save relationships but only if a couple want it to. Surveys suggest that only 9 to 23 per cent of people use counselling to get out of a relationship. One of the problems is that few couples use it at all. Only 20 per cent of divorced people tried relationship counselling before seeing a lawyer. By the time couples get to counselling their relationships are often in their death throes – studies show many of those pitching up for outside help score highly on scales of distress (i.e. they are very unhappy indeed).

There's a lot of research showing that therapy improves relationships. Relate's own surveys say that 58 per cent of their clients feel their relationships improved after counselling, and 80 per cent are satisfied with the therapy they are given. A detailed report from ACCORD, an Irish Catholic 'marriage care service' that both analysed existing research and included their own study of 1,500 couples and 1,000 individuals, also claimed success for counselling. It found that half of the men and women in their study were less stressed after counselling and that a quarter of partners improved their behaviour – in terms of being less critical, arguing less and listening more (the latter was especially an issue for men; women usually take the critical option). This sample, however, may be biased, because ACCORD is a Catholic organization with couples who may be more motivated to save their marriages.

More research comes from the highly experienced John Simons, whose review paper for the Lord Chancellor's Department is rather less optimistic. He points out that while therapy works (and the many different types have the same effects) in studies, it is less good in real life. In research studies it is not uncommon, because the conditions are not exactly the same as in usual practice (for example depressed couples may be excluded from the study to make it easier to analyse results), to find that the positive effects of treatments are inflated. Simons says that half of all couples are still distressed after the six to eight therapy sessions end. There's also a high relapse rate – couples revert to the insults and not listening after a few months of good behaviour. He cites the work of John M. Gottman, who says that relationship counselling has a limited effect – after two years it improves relationships only by 11 to 18 per cent.

Couples who come to counselling and really want to make their relationships work do better than those in less committed relationships. An Australian survey of 1,302 people in the late 1980s found that out of those who wanted to stay in a relationship 73 per cent of women and 66 per cent of men had done so. Interestingly, a quarter of men and 38 per cent of women who said they wanted to leave also remained. Couples who do less well are those who show little affection, rarely have sex and don't share housework or childcare.

So your partner is probably genuinely trying to improve your relationship, and counselling may well help to do that. You've got a lot at stake here. Given what you have to lose, how hard can it be to be less insulting and critical, to do more housework, to listen more and to be more affectionate? And it's so much better for the whole family.

REMARRIAGE RUSH

My mother died five months ago from cancer. My father, who's sixty-eight, was inconsolable but is now seeing my mother's best friend, who's divorced. I'm his youngest daughter and want him to be happy, but isn't he a bit heartless to be dating so quickly?

It's usually because widowers miss their wives so much that they look for companionship with someone else so quickly. Men often react differently from women when their partner dies. There's the myth that says women mourn for and men replace their partners. Except it's not completely a myth, because the numbers, for example in the UK from the Office for National Statistics, say that widowers are at least one and half times more likely to remarry than widows.

There are various reasons why widows are less likely to remarry – there are fewer older men for a start. But there are more subtle factors at work. A study of twenty-five widows and twenty-six widowers over the age of sixty-five, in the journal *Ageing International*, found that women mourned for longer. Both men and women didn't like feeling lonely and wanted someone to take out for supper and go on holiday with, but women preferred dating to remarriage. The reasons the women gave were similar: they'd had one happy marriage, their spouses were irreplaceable, and they didn't want to look after another man.

Men were more eager to fill the vacant position of wife and companion. Your dad just wants someone to do the things that your mother did. You may wonder if that includes sex – sometimes, and increasingly now there are drugs that can help, it does. But these older, post-bereavement relationships are more about support than passion. Even so the same success factors for relationships apply – widowers who are healthy and financially better off are more likely to meet someone else.

The need that widowers have for support is confirmed by a study of 35 widowers and 215 widows from the University of New Brunswick in the *Journal of Marriage and Family*. At six months about 15 per cent of men were dating, compared to less than 1 per cent of women, and 30 per cent of men wanted to remarry; for women it was 16 per cent. Widows got emotional support and help from friends and their children, while the widowers, in contrast, got much less. Your dad, like the widowers in this study, is looking less for someone to make the supper and more for the woman to share it with. It is the ache left by the loss of their main emotional confidante that they want to fill. Widows in this study were more likely to want someone to 'go out with' than someone to 'go home to'.

The study found that widowers with the same emotional support from friends and family as widows shared the same reduced level of need for future relationships. So your dad may be lonely despite your love and support. Please don't disapprove of his dating. Bereaved children can and do wreck these relationships. A study in the *Annals of Psychiatry* found that men and women who were dating or had remarried two years after being widowed were happier than those who weren't. Most people would want that for their fathers.

MENOPAUSAL MADNESS

I am coming up to the menopause and I am dreading it. I expect to dry up, go off sex and find that my husband has left me for someone younger. I am being serious, as this has happened to women I know. Can I do anything to stop it happening?

It's no longer politically correct to suggest that the menopause is a terrible condition for women. Didn't you know that? It's part of our life cycle, although inconveniently it comes rather early, leaving women without lubrication for at least a third of their lives. It was once thought to make women sad and stupid. In the 1960s a paper in the *Journal of the American Geriatric Society* talked about menopausal women acquiring 'a vapid cow-like feeling called a negative state'.

Menopause is defined as having not had a period for a year and usually occurs around the age of fifty, but it is preceded by a few years of hormones winding down. It's hard to see any positive effects from losing oestrogen – mood swings, an increased risk of heart disease, loss of skin elasticity, dryness in most places except when sweating from a hot flush (72 per cent of women), weight gain and anxiety. Your anxiety seems to be around your husband leaving you. Did I mention low self-esteem, another menopausal side effect? Of course, you no longer have to worry about pregnancy but will you still be having sex?

Thankfully, the research has some recommendations on how to survive the menopause, although it requires a bit of effort. You need to take exercise, keep having sex and not put on too much weight. At the risk of sounding shallow, feeling frumpy is terrible for menopausal women. It stops them having sex, which is a well-known adhesive for couples. An American study, from the Midlife Women's Health Survey, of 307 women aged between thirty-five and fifty-five found that the less attractive a woman felt, the more likely she was to have gone off sex. Around 57 per cent of women wanted less sex. The study, in the *Journal of Sex Research*, said that body fat doubles by the time women reach fifty, with waists getting thicker and breasts bigger. Oh, great. Men too, get wider, and also balder, but seem to retain their self-esteem.

Your husband is not likely to go off with someone. In fact, you're more likely to do so. In *The Female Brain*, American psychiatrist Louann Brizendine argues that 65 per cent of divorces of people over the age of fifty are initiated by women.

She says this may be due to lower oestrogen levels making them reassess their relationships (known as waking up and smelling the roses). The commonest reason for divorce in the UK is a husband's unreasonable behaviour (adultery is second but is a more common reason for husbands to divorce their wives than vice versa).

Women vary in how they go through the menopause, but most don't get depressed and do cope with the physical symptoms. If you want medical help, it's worth discussing options with your doctor, but the menopause doesn't have to be treated as a disease, so first talk to your partner, friends and family. Or, even better, talk to anyone who's been through it. You're right to think about your relationship, although maybe not so negatively. Talk to your husband, make sure you have a close, good relationship and pay attention to your sex life. If everything else was all right before the menopause, a drop in oestrogen levels won't ruin it now.

KEEPING MUM

My mother died six months ago, and I've been hurt by how unsupportive my partner has been. He was kind initially, but now he's irritated by my grief and never asks how I am. We've been together for eight years, but now I wonder if this is what he's really like. How can I get him to be more understanding?

Losing a parent is usually deeply upsetting, but not everyone understands this. Your partner may assume that as an adult you should shrug your grief off rather quickly. After all, we all know our parents are going to die, don't we? Yet the reality of that death is that it can make you sad and ill and feel unsupported. Studies say that the bereaved commonly complain of 'a difficulty getting on with people'. Combine this with findings from other studies that document how adversity of any kind tends to make relationships unhappier, and you can see the inevitability about your dissatisfaction. This is a shame, because one of the things you want from a partner is reliable support when things get tough.

Most research on what the loss of a parent does to relationships comes from America. Debra Umberson, a psychologist at Texas University, surveyed 802 people (123 bereaved and 679 non-bereaved for comparison) asking about support and 'harmony' in their relationship. In her study, published in the *Journal of Marriage and Family*, she asked how strongly people agreed with a number of statements such as 'There have been things that have happened in our relationships that I can never forgive.' The death of a mother made partners less supportive and relationships more unhappy (as did the death of a father). These effects were more pronounced in financially better off and more educated couples. The researcher suggests these couples may have been protected from nasty things and so the bereavement is more disruptive.

Umberson went on to interview seventy-three adults in depth and found general disappointment in how quickly partners expected it to be business as usual and felt inconvenienced by their partner's tears and disinclination to have sex. This sample was recruited from a notice in a newspaper and is likely to be biased in that people who volunteered to talk to a researcher may have been more distressed by either their loss or their partner's response. Certain themes, however, are supported by other research, such as a partner just not getting how it felt to lose a parent.

So it's most likely that your partner is simply underperforming as expected, rather than being 'really like' anything. Or it may be that he has never been great at talking to you, and your mother's death just makes it glaringly obvious. Some people are more naturally empathic than others – so you need to suggest to your partner how he can help you and your relationship. Tell him that you'll feel sad for a while and to bear with you, preferably with kindness. Losing a parent often makes siblings closer – so maybe you can find support elsewhere. Umberson also found that the most understanding partners had themselves lost a parent. So your partner will have the benefit of your experience when the same thing happens to him.

MANY HAPPY RETIREMENTS

My wife's retiring in a few months, and I'm worried that when she stops working she'll be lost. She's always worked full time, even after we had children. She's hinting that I could retire too (although I wouldn't get a pension yet). I don't know any retired couples – is it difficult to get used to? We used to joke about longing for retirement but it doesn't seem so funny now.

People generally have mixed feelings about retiring. Psychologists say it's a time of transition that continues for months after the multiple send offs with their presents (often related to a hobby) and embarrassing speeches. When you retire you lose your job, the money that goes with it and the routine that finds you crushed on a commuter train each morning. Traditionally, men suffered the most from this, but more recent research (quoted by the Policy Studies Institute) suggests it can hurt women more, because with career breaks for children they feel there's more they could have achieved in their working lives.

The Policy Studies Institute (in their own study) asked forty-eight men and women how they'd coped with retirement and found the happiest people were those in couples who had strong ideas about what they wanted to do and saw retirement as an opportunity to see friends and develop interests. Having enough money and being in good health increased the chances of a happy retirement.

The stereotype of retired men getting under the feet of their long-suffering wives may be less common now, but the problem remains. When one and later both of you are at home all day, what does this do to your relationship? Ideally, you should have started talking about this five years ago, planning what you'll do both together and apart (bridge and cruises are good, but there are many other things you can do, including voluntary work) and how you will pay for it. Of course, if you are leaving a stressful job you may find that retirement improves your relationship enormously.

Even so, it is likely to take time to settle after retirement. The research shows that although couples eventually make this adjustment they row more in the first two years of retiring. A study from La Trobe University in Australia using data on over 300 married people found that some had a honeymoon period after retirement while others had more of a trough. However, generally the better and worse times evened out until after three years, when nearly half the couples said they were happier in retirement. Couples who retire together may find it easier to adjust because they automatically have a companion whose life has changed in the same way. Couples in the study by the Policy Studies Institute said that after retiring together they grew closer and happier.

You need to start talking about both of your retirement plans. Immediately would be good. If you don't want to retire yet, be clear about this, as being pushed into it will damage your relationship. Don't worry, your wife will find things to do, but her retiring will take time for both of you to get used to. It's not a one-off event but the rest of your lives.

ACHE OF HEARTS

My grandmother died after a short illness, and my grandfather was taken ill shortly afterwards with high blood pressure and heart trouble. We think he doesn't want to go on living without her, and although we go round and look after him, he is clearly unhappy and frail. Is it true you can die from a broken heart?

A broken heart is not just a figure of speech, it's a genuine medical emergency. It was the *New England Medical Journal,*

not given to flights of fancy, that coined the term Broken Heart Syndrome. Other medical journals, too, have described cases of people who have died suddenly from heart attacks after traumatic events. It seems that you can either die from a broken heart or from being scared to death; the mechanism is much the same. People usually get chest pain and feel breathless, just as if they're having a heart attack. Something happens to your heart to disrupt the normal beating of its muscle, specifically in the area of the chunky left ventricle (lower left chamber), which pushes blood out round the body. Dr Ilan S. Wittstein from Johns Hopkins University School of Medicine estimates that 2 per cent of people with heart attack symptoms have broken heart syndrome, which is a lot of sad or frightened people, because heart attacks are common. In a review of the research in this area nearly 90 per cent of broken hearts occurred in women (wouldn't you just know it), particularly in those between fifty-eight and seventy-seven years of age. Maybe your grandfather has a softer heart than most.

The cause of this broken heart syndrome is thought to be a surge in stress hormones such as adrenaline, which stun the heart, although it's not clear how they do this. This is a different scenario from your average heart attack, which is due to blocked arteries cutting off the blood supply to the heart muscle. But the good news is that people recover well: only 3.5 per cent will have another attack.

This doesn't mean, however, that the loss of a loved one can't have a lasting, negative impact on your health. A study in the *British Medical Journal* in 1969 followed up 4,486 widowers of fifty-five and over and found that 213 died within the first six months of their wife dying, 40 per cent above the expected rate for married men of that age. Most died of heart disease (common things being common) but these death rates returned to normal after six months. Another study of 903 relatives of patients dying in a semi-rural part of Wales found that 4.8 per cent died within a year, compared to 0.68 per cent of people who hadn't lost a relative. The difference was most profound among widows and widowers, who had ten times the death rate (mostly from heart disease) of people who hadn't lost their spouse. However, once again the physical trauma was relatively short-lived. After the first year the rates returned to normal.

Widowers tend to do worse than widows because they are more socially isolated and get less support from friends and family. Depression is common in widowers too, and this will make your grandfather less able to look after himself. Try to get him to eat healthily and do something active. The risk of dying from a broken heart may be greatest early on, and if you can get your grandfather through the first difficult year, he may still be sad but physically he'll be in better shape.

EVERLASTING LOVE

I've been with my partner for ten years and we have two children under ten. Our relationship has got less passionate and more routine. What's our relationship going to be like in twenty to thirty years' time? How can we manage to stay together and not be bored with each other?

The path of happiness in relationships follows a U-shaped curve. Happiness falls rapidly in the first years of a relationship, plateaus and then climbs again, usually once the children leave home. Some research shows this curve occurs without children. This suggests that couples in the twilight of their years (or sagging middle age) enjoy their relationships more than they did when they were young. But does this mean they're having a great time or saying, 'We're stuck with each other; let's make the best of it'?

The ingredients for a happy relationship are well known. John M. Gottman, in his 'Love Lab', has analysed video interactions of thousands of couples and identified the characteristics of those relationships likely to survive versus those that won't. His research papers show his predictions are correct over 90 per cent of the time.

Firstly you have to deal with conflict. If you criticize, act defensively, absent yourself (emotionally) or show contempt for your partner, then your relationship is doomed. On the plus side you can get away with anything if you say it in a warm, positive way. Perhaps your partner comes home, slumps in front of the television and barely acknowledges you or the children. Now, you could say, 'You selfish pig, you always sit in front of the television, you don't even say hello to me or the kids, you're a useless dad.' This is what Gottman calls a 'harsh start up'. Compare a soft start up: 'It's lovely to see you, and it would really help me if you could play with the children while I finish up here.' Now guess which one works better. Gottman advises a ratio of saying five positive to one negative thing to your partner, which could be challenging. Using humour, which is also effective in lightening up relationships and diffusing conflict, may be more achievable.

So what about boredom? You need to do new and, I'm sorry to say, exciting things together. You must set aside time to go out, as a couple, on your own, not with more interesting couples. A study of eighty-seven married couples who had been together for fifteen years, in the 1980s, found they were good friends, enjoyed each other's company and depended on each other. Researchers were struck by how affectionate the couples were to each other. And affection doesn't have to be a euphemism for 'no sex'. A recent study from the *British Medical Journal* of 1,506 adults aged seventy from Gothenburg in Sweden found that the percentage of people saying their sex lives were good had increased between 1971 to 2001. The percentage of sexually happy men in this study rose from 40 to 57 per cent and that of women from 35 to 52 per cent.

Most long-term relationships seem to be happy. A study of 351 long-term couples in 1986 by researchers from the Southern Illinois University at Edwardsville found that 300 were happy. One husband told the researchers. 'Commitment means a willingness to be unhappy for a while. You're not going to be happy with each other all the time.'

Sources

1. MR OR MRS RIGHT

Chat-up Lies

'Chat-up Lines as Male Sexual Displays', Christopher Bale, Rory Morrison, Peter G. Caryl, *Personality and Individual Differences* 40 (2006), 655–64

Online Mating

'Managing Impressions Online: Self-presentation Processes in the Online Dating Environment', Nicole Ellison, Rebecca Heino, Jennifer Gibbs, *Journal of Computer-Mediated Communication* 11, 2 (2006)

'An Exploration of Identity Re-creation in the Context of Internet Dating', Jennifer Yurichisin, Kittichai Watchravespringkan, Deborah Brown McRae, *Social Behaviour and Personality* 33, 8 (2005), 735–50

Press release, University of Bath: www.bathac.uk/pr/releases/internet-dating.htm

Pew Internet and American Life Project. Online Dating: http://www.pewinternet.org/pdfs/PIP_Online_Dating.pdf

Speedy Dating

'HurryDate: Mate Preferences in Action', Robert Kurzban, Jason Weeden, *Evolution and Human Behavior* 26 (2005), 227–44

'Speed-dating as an Invaluable Tool for Studying Romantic Attraction: A Methodological Primer', Eli J. Finkle, Paul W. Eastwick, J. Matthews, *Personal Relationships* 14, 1 (2007)

'Can Anyone Be "The" One? Evidence on Mate Selection from Speed Dating', Michele Belot, Marco Francesconi, University of Essex Discussion Paper (2006)

Romantic Timing
'Spring's not the Favourite Season nor a Time for Love', Scripps Howard
News Service, newspolls.org (2003)

In the Stars?
'Ten Million Marriages: A Test of Astrological "Love Signs"', David Voas,
University of Manchester (2007)

Birth Order
'Birth Order, Sibling Sex Ratio, Handedness, and Sexual Orientation of
Male and Female Participants in a BBC Internet Research Project', Ray
Blanchard, Richard A. Lippa, *Archives of Sexual Behaviour* 36, 2 (2007),
163–76

'Birth Order and Sexual Strategy', Richard L. Michalski, Todd K.
Shackleford, *Personality and Individual Differences* 33, 4 (2002), 661–7

Wanted: Handsome Men
'Beautiful Parents Have More Daughters: A Further Implication of the
Generalized Trivers-Willard Hypothesis', Satoshi Kanazawa, *Journal of
Theoretical Biology* 244 (2007), 133–40

Reeling from Rejection
'The Self-fulfilling Prophecy in Close Relationships: Rejection Sensitivity
and Rejection by Romantic Partners', Geraldine Downey, Antonio L.
Freitas, Benjamin Michaelis, Hala Khouri, *Journal of Personality and Social
Psychology* 75, 2 (1998), 545–60

'Adult Attachment Style. 1: Its Relationship to Clinical Depression',
A. Bifulco, P. M. Moran, C. Ball, O. Bernazzani, *Social Psychiatry and
Psychiatric Epidemiology* 37, 2 (2002), 50–59

'Implications of Rejection Sensitivity for Intimate Relationships',
Geraldine Downey, Scott I. Feldman, *Journal of Personality and Social
Psychology* 70, 6 (1996), 1327–43

Nice Guy But...
'Physical Attractiveness and the "Nice Guy Paradox": Do Nice Guys
Really Finish Last?', Geoffrey C. Urbaniak, *Sex Roles* 49 (2003)

'Young Women's Dating Behavior: Why/Why Not Date a Nice Guy?',
Anita K. McDaniel, *Sex Roles* 53 (2005), 347–59

Blonde or Brunette?
'How Do Men Feel about Women's Hair Colour?: A Survey of Male
Attitudes and Reactions to Women's Hair', Peter Ayton, City University
(unpublished)

'The Influence of Skin Tone, Hair Length, and Hair Colour on Ratings of Women's Physical Attractiveness, Health and Fertility', Viren Swami, Adrian Furnham, Kiran Joshi, *Scandinavian Journal of Psychology* 49, 5 (2008)

'European Hair and Eye Color. A Case of Frequency-dependent Sexual Selection?', Peter Frost, *Evolution and Human Behavior* 27, 2 (2006), 85–103

Dim View
'A Susceptibility Locus for Myopia in the Normal Population is Linked to the PAX6 Gene Region on chromosome 11: A Genomewide Scan of Dizygotic Twins', C. J. Hammond, Toby Andrew, Ying Tat Mak, Tim D. Spector, *American Journal of Human Genetics* 75, 2 (2004), 294–304

'Genes and Environment in Refractive Error: The Twin Eye Study', C. J. Hammond, H. Snieder, Clare E. Gilbert, Tim D. Spector, *Investigative Ophthalmology and Visual Science* 42, 6 (2001), 1232–6.

Big Egos
'Narcissism and Resistance to Doubts about Romantic Partners', Joshua D. Foster, W. Keith Campbell, *Journal of Research in Personality* 39, 5 (2005), 550–57

'Narcissism and Commitment in Romantic Relationships: An Investment Model Analysis', W. Keith Campbell, Craig A. Foster, *Personality and Social Psychology Bulletin* 28, 4 (2002), 484–95

'Assessing Commitment in Personal Relationships', Scott M. Stanley, Howard J. Markman, *Journal of Marriage and Family*, 54 (1992), 595–608

Freudian Blip
Why Smart Men Marry Smart Women, Christine B. Whelan, Simon and Schuster, 2006

'Facialmetric Similarities Mediate Mate Choice: Sexual Imprinting on Opposite-sex Parents', T. Bereczkei, Gabor Hegedus, Gabor Hajnal, *Proceedings of the Royal Society B.* (2008)

'Homogamy, Genetic Similarity, and Imprinting: Parental Influence on Mate Choice Preferences', T. Bereczkei, P. Gyuris, P. Koves, L. Bernath, *Personality and Individual Differences* 33, 5 (2002), 677–90

2. OPPORTUNITY KNOCKS

Poached Partners
'Nifty Ways to Leave Your Lover: The Tactics People Use to Entice and Disguise the Process of Human Mate Poaching', David P. Schmitt, Todd

K. Shackleford, *Personality and Social Psychology Bulletin* 29, 8 (2003), 1018–35

'Patterns and Universals of Mate Poaching Across 53 Nations: The Effects of Sex, Culture, and Personality on Romantically Attracting Another Person's Partner', David P. Schmitt and 121 members of the International Sexuality Description Project, *Journal of Personality and Social Psychology* 86, 4 (2004), 560–84

Office Romance
Office Romance: Love, Power and Sex in the Workplace, Lisa A. Mainiero, Rawson Associates, 1989

'Frisky Business', Mary Loftus, *Psychology Today* March/April 1995

'Office Romance', in *Encyclopedia of Small Businesses*, Endnotes.com: www.enotes.com/small-business-encyclopedia/office-romance

One Night Only
'Gender and Sexual Standards in Dating Relationships', Laura Bettor, Susan S. Hendrick, Clyde Hendrick, *Personal Relationships* 2, 4 (1995), 359–69

'Predicting Intentions to Engage in Casual Sex', Edward S. Herold, Eleanor Maticka-Tyndale, Dawn Mewhinney, *Journal of Social and Personal Relationships* 15, 4 (1998), 502–16

'Sex Differences in Regret: All for Love or Some for Lust?', Neal J. Rose, Ginger L. Pennington, Jill Coleman, Maria Janicki, Norman P. Li, Douglas T. Kennick, *Personality and Social Psychology Bulletin* 2, 6 (2006), 770–80

'Women and One-night Stands', Sharon Hinchliff, presented at the British Psychological Society's Annual Conference, March 2006

Poles Apart
'Two of a Kind: Perceptions of Own and Partner's Attachment Characteristics', Anna P. Puvolo, Lisa A. Fabin, *Personal Relationships* 6, 1 (1999), 57–79

'Assortative Mating and Marital Quality in Newlyweds: A Couple-centered Approach', Shanhong Luo, Eva C. Klohnen, *Journal of Personality and Social Psychology* 88, 2 (2005), 304–26

'Romantic Mood Induction and Attraction to a Dissimilar Other: Is Love Blind?', Joel A. Gold, Richard M. Ryckman, Norman R. Mosley, *Personality and Social Psychology Bulletin* 10, 3 (1984), 358–68

Tall Story
'Women's Height, Reproductive Success and the Evolution of Sexual Dimorphism in Modern Humans', D. Nettle, Proceedings of the Royal Society of London, 2002

'Attractiveness and Height: The Role of Stature in Dating Preference, Frequency of Dating, and Perceptions of Attractiveness', James A. Shepperd and Alan J. Strathman, *Personality and Social Psychology Bulletin* 15, 4 (1989), 617–27

First Mover
'Who's Going to Make the First Move? Pluralistic Ignorance as an Impediment to Relationship Formation', Jacquie D. Vorauer, Rebecca K. Ratner, *Journal of Social and Personal Relationships* 13, 4 (1996), 483–506

Wish You Were Here
'"What happens in Tenerife stays in Tenerife": Understanding Women's Sexual Behaviour on Holiday', Michelle Thomas, *Culture, Health and Sexuality* 7, 6 (2005), 571–84

'Sexual Relationships on Holiday: A Case of Situational Disinhibition?', J. Richard Eiser, Nicholas Ford, *Journal of Social and Personal Relationships* 12, 3 (1995), 323–39

'The Summer Holiday', MORI: http://extranet.ipsos-mori.com/polls/1998/nfm3.shtml

Ex or Hex?
'Poaching, Promiscuity, and Deceit: Combating Mating Rivalry in Same-sex Friendships', April L. Bleske, Todd K. Shackleford, *Personal Relationships* 8, 4 (2005), 407–24

'Nifty Ways to Leave Your Lover: The Tactics People Use to Entice and Disguise the Process of Human Mate Poaching', David P. Schmitt, Todd K. Shackleford, *Personality and Social Psychology Bulletin* 29, 8 (2003), 1018–35

'Patterns and Universals of Mate Poaching Across 53 Nations: The Effects of Sex, Culture, and Personality on Romantically Attracting Another Person's Partner', David P. Schmitt and 121 members of the International Sexuality Description Project, *Journal of Personality and Social Psychology* 86, 4 (2004), 560–84

Unsettling Thoughts
'What if You Can't Get What You Want? Willingness to Compromise Ideal Mate Selection Standards as a Function of Sex, Mate Value, and Relationship Context', Pamela C. Regan, *Personality and Social Psychology Bulletin* 24, 12 (1998), 1294–303

'An Iconic Report 20 Years Later: Many of Those Women Married After All': WSJ.com/public/article/SB114852493706762691.html

'Age at Marriage and Marital Instability: Revisiting the Becker-Landes-Michael Hypothesis', Evelyn L. Lehrer, *Journal of Population Economics* 21, 2 (2008)

Biographical Determinants of Marital Quality, C. Ayles, One Plus One, 2004

Relationships Indicators Survey 2006, Robyn Parker, Australian Institute of Family Studies, 2006

As Marriage and Parenthood Drift Apart, Public is Concerned about Social Impact, PewResearchCenter Publications, 2007

Rebound to Fail?
'Does the Rebound Effect Exist? Time to Remarriage and Subsequent Union Stability', Nicholas H. Wolfinger, *Journal of Divorce and Remarriage* 46 (2007), 9–20

Surviving the Breakup: How Children and Parents Cope with Divorce, J. S. Wallerstein, J. B. Kelly, Basic Books, 1980

'Trying Again: Repartnering after Dissolution of a Union', John Ermisch, ISER Working Papers no. 2002–19

3. AFTER THE FIRST FEW DATES

Can't Hurry Love
personal communication, Robert Milardo, University of Maine

Romantic Love, C. Hendricks, Sage, 1992

Friendly Fire
'The Influence of Parents and Friends on the Quality and Stability of Romantic Relationships: A Three-wave Longitudinal Investigation', Susan Sprecher, Diane Femlee, *Journal of Marriage and Family* 54 (1992), 888–900

'Marginalised Relationships: The Impact of Social Disapproval on Romantic Relationship Commitment', Justin J. Lehmiller, Christopher R. Agnew, *Personality and Psychology Bulletin* 32 (2006), 40–51

Round the Bend
Sex Differences in Driving and Insurance Risk, Social Issues Research Centre, August 2004

'Women Drivers "better" claim proved': news.bbc.co.uk/1 /hi/wales/1590309.stm

'Men Driving Women Around the Bend on British Roads', ICM survey
for MissMotors.co.uk: icmresearch.co.uk

'Predicting Change in Marital Satisfaction from Husbands' and Wives'
Conflict Resolution Styles', Lawrence A. Kurdek, *Journal of Marriage and
Family* 57, 1 (1995), 153–64

'Are Female Drivers Safer? An Application of the Decomposition
Method', Guohua Li, Susan P. Baker, Jean A. Langlois, Gabor D. Kelen,
Epidemiology 9, 4 (1998), 379–384

Split the Difference?
'Predictors of Divorce Adjustment: Stressors, Resources, and Definitions',
Hongyu Wang, Paul R. Armato, *Journal of Marriage and Family* 62, 3
(2004)

'Divorce and Remarriage in England and Wales', John Haskey, *Population
Trends* 95 (1999)

'The Male Way of Mourning Divorce: When, What and How', Nehami
Baum, *Clinical Social Work Journal* 31, 1 (2003)

Romeo and Juliet
'The Adversity of Secret Relationships', Craig A. Foster, W. Keith
Campbell, *Personal Relationship* 12 (2005), 125–43

'Revealing and not Revealing the Status of Romantic Relationships to
Social Networks, Leslie A. Baxter, Sally Widenmann, *Journal of Social and
Personal Relationships* 10 (1993), 321–36

Controlling the Remote
'Couples Watching Television: Gender, Power and the Remote Control',
Alexis J. Walker, *Journal of Marriage and Family* 58 (1996), 813–23

Family Television: Cultural Power and Domestic Leisure, David Morley,
Routledge, 1986

Sex and Lies
'Truth and Consequences: Using the Bogus Pipeline to Examine Sex
Differences in Self-reported Sexuality', Michele G. Alexander, Terri D.
Fisher, *Journal of Sex Research* 40 (2003), 27

'Estimating Number of Lifetime Sexual Partners: Men and Women Do
it Differently', Norman R. Brown, Robert C. Sinclair, *Journal of Sex
Research* 36 (1999)

'Prostitution and the Sex Discrepancy in Reported Number of Sexual
Partners', Devon D. Brewer, John J. Potterat, Sharon B. Garrett, Stephen
Q Muth, John M. Roberts Jr, Danuta Kasprzyk, Daniel E. Montano,

William W. Darrow, *Proceedings of the National Academy of Sciences* 97, 22 (2000), 12385–8

'The Gender Discrepancy in Reported Number of Sexual Partners: Effects of Anonymity', Lindsay A. Wittrock, *Journal of Undergraduate Research* 7 (2004)

'Preferred Level of Sexual Experience in a Date or Mate: The Merger of Two Methodologies', Susan Sprecher, Pamela C. Regan, Kathleen McKinney, Kallye Maxwell, Robert Wazienski, *Journal of Sex Research* 34, 4 (1997), 327–37

Kiss Off
Kissing, Andrea Demirjian, Penguin, 2006

'Sex Differences in Romantic Kissing Among College Students: An Evolutionary Perspective', Susan M. Hughes, Marissa A. Harrison, Gordon G. Gallup Jr, *Evolutionary Psychology* 5, 3 (2007)

I Was Only Saying…
'Forgiveness in Marriage: Current Status and Future Directions', Frank F. Fisham, Julie Hall, Steven R.H. Beach, *Family Relations* 55, 4 (2006), 415–27

'Fire and Ice in Marital Communications: Hostile and Distancing Behaviours as Predictors of Marital Distress', Linda J. Roberts, *Journal of Marriage and Family* 62 (2000), 693–707

'Decade Review: Observing Marital Interaction', *Journal of Marriage and Family* 62 (2000):927–94

4. WHAT HAPPENS NEXT?

Going the Distance
http//www.longdistancerelationships.net/about_the_center.htm

'Living Love at Long-Distance: Intimacy in Couples Who Live Apart', Mary Holmes, *Economic and Social Research Council*, RES-000–22–0351 (2006)

Homeward Bound
'Idealization, Reunions, and Stability in Long-distance Dating Relationships', Laura Stafford, Andy J. Merolla, *Journal of Social and Personal Relationships* 24, 1 (2007), 37–54

'When Long-distance Dating Partners become Geographically Close', Laura Stafford, Andy J. Merolla, Janessa D. Castle, *Journal of Social and Personal Relationships* 23, 6 (2006), 901–19

Faith in Our Relationship
Inter-ethnic marriage, National Statistics, www.statistics.gov.uk, 2006

'Convergence and Divergence in Ethnic Divorce Patterns: A Research Note', F. L. Jones, *Journal of Marriage and Family* 58 (1996), 213–18

Toy Boy or not Toy Boy?
'The Age Difference at Marriage in England and Wales: A Century of Patterns and Trends', *Population Trends* 120 (2005)

'Women Marrying Younger Men, England and Wales'. One Plus One: www.oneplusone.org.uk/ICOR/StatisticsDetails.php?Ref=44

'Age Differences Between Sexual Partners in the United States', Jacqueline E. Darroch, David J. Landry, Selene Oslak, *Family Planning Perspectives* 31, 4 (1999)

'Cougars and their Cubs', AARP.org: www.aarp.org/family/love/articles/cougars_and_their.html

My Valentine
'Valentine's Day Romance', survey by Blue Nile: *www.bluenile.com*

'Lifestyles Condoms Valentine's Day Survey' by Harris Interactive

'Ideal couples and romance' *Psychology Today* accessed at http://www.psychologytoday.com/articles/index.php?/term=pto-19950301-000027&pr

Stop or Shop
'The Process of Entering in to Cohabiting Unions'. Sharon Sassler, *Journal of Marriage and Family*, Vol 66 Issue 2, May 2004, 491–506

Too Many Cooks
'Commitment in Polyamorous Relationships', Elaine Cook, *www.aphroweb.com* 2005

'Open Marriages and Marital Adjustment', Dale Wachowiak, Hannelore Bragg, *Journal of Marriage and the Family*, February 1980, 57–62

'What Psychology Professionals Should Know About Polyamory', Geri D. Weitzman, *www.polyamory.org/-joe/polypaper.htm*

He's not the One
'The State of Our Unions 2001'. The National Marriage Project. Rutgers, The State University of New Jersey.

'Creating Mr Right and Ms Right: Interpersonal ideals and personal change in newlyweds', Ann. P. Ruvolo, Catherine M. Ruvolo, *Personal Relationships*, 7 200 341–362

'Falling in love for all the right reasons', Dr Neil Clark Warren, Hachette Group Book USA 2005

Getting to 'Yes'
'Commitment Processes in Accounts of the Development of Premarital relationships', Catherine A. Surra, Debra K. Hughes, *Journal of Marriage and Family* 59 February 1997 5–21

'Communication Strategies for Intensifying Dating Relationships: Identification, Use and Structure'. James H. Tolhuizen, *Journal of Social and Personal Relationships*, 1989; 6; 4113

'Frequently asked questions about commitment'. National Healthy Marriage Resource Center www.healthymarriageinfo.org/research

Marry Without Haste
'Sliding Versus Deciding: Inertia and the Premarital Cohabiting Effect', Scott M. Stanley, Galena Kline Rhoades, Howard J. Markman, *Family Relations*, 55 October 2006, 499–509

'Married or not in Britain today', One Plus One (*www.oneplusone.org.uk*)

Focus on Families, 2007 edition, Palgrave Macmillan (available fwww. statistics.gov.uk/focuson/families)

'Premarital Cohabitation and Subsequent Marital Stability', David de Vaus, Lixia Qu, Ruth Weston, *Family Matters* 65 (2003)

Cohabitation and Marriage: How are they Related?, Anne-Marie Ambert, Vanier Institute of the Family, 2006

'The Relationship Between Cohabitation and Marital Quality and Stability: Change Across Cohorts?', Claire M. Kamp Dush, Catherine L. Cohan, Paul R. Amato, *Journal of Marriage and Family* 65, 3 (2003), 539–50

Love Match has Catch
Stochastic Models of Decision Making in Arranged Marriages, Amitrajeet A. Batabyal, University Press of America, 2006

'Love Matches and Arranged Marriages: A Chinese Replication', Xu Xiaohe, Martin King Whyte, *Journal of Marriage and Family* 52, 3 (1990), 709–22

'Divorce Rate in India', Divorcerate.org: www.divorcerate.org/divorce-rate-in-india.html

'40% Divorce Rate in Mumbai, India', South Asia Connection: www. southasianconnection.com/blogs/607/40-Divorce-Rate-In-Mumbai-India

What's in a Name?
'The Surname of Married Women in the European Union', Marie-France
Valetas, *Population and Societies* 367 (2001)

'Making a Name: Women's Surnames at Marriage and Beyond', Claudia
Goldin, Maria Shim, *Journal of Economic Perspectives* 18, 2 (2004), 143–60

Looking Good?
'Facial Resemblance in Engaged and Married Couples', Verlin B. Hinsz,
Journal of Social and Personal Relationships 6, 2 (1989), 223–9

'Physical Attractiveness and Courtship Progress', Gregory L. White,
Journal of Personality and Social Psychology 39, 4 (1980), 660–68

'Beyond Initial Attraction: Physical Attractiveness in Newlywed Marriage',
James K. McNulty, Lisa A. Neff, Benjamin R. Karney, *Journal of Family
Psychology* 22, 1 (2008), 133–43

5. JEALOUSY AND AFFAIRS

Men in Uniform
'The Remains of the Workday: Impact of Job Stress and Exhaustion on
Marital Interaction in Police Couples', Nicole A. Roberts, Robert W.
Levenson, *Journal of Marriage and Family* 63, 4 (2001), 10052–67

'Managing Stress and Traumatic Stress Incidents', Corneil Askew,
an Applies paper submitted to the Department of Interdisciplinary
Technology, 2004

'Medical Speciality and the Incidence of Divorce', *New England Journal of
Medicine* 336 (1997), 800–803

New Company
'Working Late: Do Workplace Sex Ratios Affect Partnership Formation
and Dissolution?', Michael Svarer, *Journal of Human Resources* 42, 3
(2007)

Work–Love Balance, a research report by Derek Kemp, Human and Legal
Resources Limited, 2004

Is She Faithful?
'Predictors of Young Dating Adults' Inclination to Engage in Extradyadic
Sexual Activities: A Multi-perspective Study', Anna R. McAlister, Nancy
Pachana, Chris J. Jackson, *British Journal of Psychology* 96, 3 (2005),
331–50

'Infidelity', Menstuff: www.menstuff.org/issues/byissue/infidelity.html
(2008)

'Your Unadulterated Thoughts on Adultery', MSNBC: www.msnbc.msn. com/id/18055526 (2007)

The Handbook of Divorce and Romantic Dissolution, eds. M. Fine, J. Harvey, Psychology Press, 2005

Me or the Missus?
Quiet Desperation: The Truth About Successful Men, Jan Halper, Warner Books, 1988

Affair-proof Your Marriage, Lana Staheli, Harper Perennial, 1998

Private Lies: Infidelity and the Betrayal of Intimacy, Frank Pittman, Norton, 1989

Is He Cheating On You?: 829 Telltale Signs, Lifestyle Publications, 2002

Green-eyed Monster
'The Role of Relationship Development and Attachment in the Experience of Romantic Jealousy', Leanne K. Knobloch, Denise Haunani Solomon, Michael G. Cruz, *Personal Relationships* 8m 2 (2001), 205–34

'Emotional and Behavioral Responses to Romantic Jealousy Expressions', Stephen M. Yoshimura, *Communication Reports* 17, 2 (2004)

'Reactions to Hypothetical Jealousy-producing Events', Gary L. Hansen, *Family Relations* 31, 4 (1982), 510–18

Flirt Alert
'Tickling the Monster: Jealousy Induction in Relationships', Amy A. Fleischmann, Brian H. Spitzberg, Peter A. Anderson, Scott C. Roesch, *Journal of Social and Personal Relationships* 22, 1 (2005), 49–73

'Cyber-flirting: An Examination of Men's and Women's Flirting Behaviour Both offline and on the Internet', Monica T. Whitty, *Behaviour Change* 21, 2 (2004), 115–27

SIRC Guide to Flirting, Kate Fox, Social Issues Research Centre: www. sirc.org/publik/flirt.html

Truth or Dare?
'Identity Concerns Following a Severe Relational Transgression: The Role of Discovery Method for the Relational Outcomes of Infidelity', Walid A., Afifi, Wendy L. Falato, Judith L. Weiner, *Journal of Social and Personal Relationships* 18,2 (2001), 291–308

'Communicative Infidelity', M. A. Tafoya, B. H. Spitzberg, in *The Dark Side of Interpersonal Communication* (2nd ed.), B. H. Spitzberg, W. R. Cupach (eds.). Lawrence Erlbaum Associates, 2007, 199–242.

Just Good Friends
'"We're Just Friends": Myth Construction as a Communication Strategy in Communicating Cross-sex Friendships', Vickie Harvey, *Qualitative Report* 8,2 (2003), 314–32

'Can Men and Women Just be Friends?', April L. Bleske, David M. Buss, *Personal Relationships*, 7, 2 (2000), 131–51

6. BREAK-UPS OR MAKE-UPS?

Revenge is Sour
'Goals and Emotional Outcomes of Revenge Activities in Interpersonal Relationships', Stephen Yoshimura, *Journal of Social and Personal Relationships* 24, 1 (2007), 8

Post traumatic love disorder
'Whose Decision Was it? The Effects of Initiator Status on Adjustment to Marital Disruption', Ellen J. Pettit, Bernard L. Bloom, *Journal of Marriage and Family* 46, 3 (1984), 587–95

'What is Posttraumatic Stress Disorder?', Y. Arieh, J. Shalev, *Clinical Psychiatry* 62, suppl. 17 (2001), 4–10

'The Effects of Marital and Nonmarital Union Transition on Health', Zheng Wu, Randy Hart, *Journal of Marriage and Family* 64, 2 (2002), 420–33

Tears Before Bedtime
'Regional Brain Activity in Women Grieving a Romantic Relationship Breakup'. A. Najib, J. P. Lorberbaum, S. Kose, D. E. Binning, M. S. George, *American Journal of Psychiatry* 161 (2004), 2245–56

Unfair Affair
'Unrequited Love: On Heartbreak, Anger, Guilt, Scriptlessness, and Humiliation', Roy F. Baumeister, Sara R. Wotman, Arlene M. Stillwell, *Journal of Personality and Social Psychology* 64, 3 (1993), 377–94

'Motivations for Unreciprocated Love', Arthur Aron, Elaine N. Aron, Josephine Allen, *Personality and Social Psychology Bulletin* 24, 8 (1998), 787–96

Cuddling Deficiency
'Investigating the Behavioral Indicators of Relational Commitment', Daniel J. Weigel, Deborah S. Ballard-Reisch, *Journal of Social and Personal Relationships* 19, 3 (2002), 403–23

'The Waxing and Waning of Relational Intimacy: Touch as a Function of Relational Stage, Gender and Touch Avoidance', Laura K. Guerrero,

Peter A. Andersen, *Journal of Social and Personal Relationships* 8, 2 (1991), 147–165

Alpha Male Alert
'Avoidance of Intimacy: An Attachment Perspective', Kim Bartholomew, *Journal of Social and Personal Relationships* 7, 2 (1990), 147–75

'The Importance of Similarity and Understanding of Partners' Marital Ideals to Relationship Satisfaction', Linda K. Acitelli, David A. Kenny, Debra Weiner, *Personal Relationships* 8, 2 (2001), 167–85

'Cognitive Processes Underlying Human Mate Choice: The Relationship Between Self-perception and Mate Preference in Western Society', Peter M. Buston, Stephen T. Emlen, *Proceedings of the National Academy of Sciences* 100, 15 (2003), 8805–10

Gone for Good?
'Whose Decision Was It?: The Effect of Initiator Status on Adjustment to Marital Disruption', E. J. Pettit, B. L. Bloom, *Journal of Marriage and Family* 46, 3 (1994), 587–96

'Separations, Reconciliations and Living Apart in Cohabiting and Marital Union', Georgina Binstock, Arland Thornton, *Journal of Marriage and Family* 65, 2 (2003), 432–43

'The Dissolution of Romantic Relationships: Factors Involved in Relationship Stability and Emotional Distress', Jeffry A. Simpson, *Journal of Personality and Social Psychology* October 53, 4 (1987), 683–92

Gullible or Gutted?
www.straightspouse.org

'Heterosexual Women's Perceptions of Their Marriages to Bisexual or Homosexual Men', Dorothea Hays, Aurele Samuels, *Journal of Homosexuality* 18 (1989), 81–100

'Sexual Behaviour in Britain: Partnerships, Practices, and HIV Risk Behaviours', Anne Johnson, Catherine H. Mercer, Bob Erens, Andrew J. Copas, Sally McManus, Kaye Wellings *et al.*, *The Lancet* 358 (2001), 1835–42

'Married Homosexual Men: Prevalence and Background', Michael W. Ross, *Marriage and Family Review* 14 (1989), p. 35

'Paths and Pitfalls: How Heterosexual Spouses Cope when their Husbands or Wives Come Out', in J. J. Bigner, J. L. Wetchler, *Relationship Therapy with Same-sex Couples*, Haworth Press, 2004

'When a Spouse Comes Out as Gay, Lesbian or Bisexual', A. P. Buxton, in J. J. Bigner (ed.) *An Introduction to GLBT Family Studies*, Haworth Press, 2006, 67–88

'Modes of adjustments of married homosexuals', H. Laurence Ross, *Social Problems* 18, 3, 187, 385–93

In the Genes?
'The Long Reach of Divorce: Divorce and Child Well-being Across Three Generations', Paul R. Amato, Jacob Cheadle, *Journal of Family and Marriage* 67, 1 (2005), 191–206

'Parental Divorce and Interpersonal Trust in Adult Offspring', Valerie King, *Journal of Marriage and Family* 64, 3 (2002), 642–56

'The Transmission of Marital Instability Across Generations: Relationship Skills or Commitment to Marriage?', Paul R. Amato, Danelle D. DeBoer, *Journal of Marriage and Family* 63, 4 (2001), 1038–51

'Parental Divorce and Premarital Couples: Commitment and Other Relationship Characteristics', Susan E. Jacques, Catherine A. Surra, *Journal of Marriage and Family* 63, 4 (2001), 627–39

Third Time Lucky?
'Changing Patterns of Remarriage', Larry Bumpass, James Sweet, Teresa Castro Martin. *Journal of Marriage and Family*, 52, 747–56 (1990), 747–56

One Plus One, Frequently Asked Questions: www.oneplusone.org.uk/faqs.asp

'The Marital Happiness of Remarried Divorced Persons', Norval D. Glenn, Charles N Weaver, *Journal of Marriage and Family* May 39, 2 (1977), 331–7

'Reinvestigating Remarriage: Another Decade of Progress', Marilyn Coleman, Lawrence Ganong, Mark Fine, *Journal of Marriage and Family* 62, 4 (2000), 1288–307

7. SEX LIVES

Tri-weekly
'Sexual Satisfaction and Sexual Self-disclosure Within Dating Relationships', E. Sandra Byers, Stephanie Demmons, *Journal of Sex Research* 36, 2 (1999), 180–89

'The Saliency of Sexuality in the Early Years of Marriage', Cathy Stein Greenblat, *Journal of Marriage and Family* 45, 2 (1993), 289–99

Try Weekly
'Sexual Dysfunction in the United States', Edward O. Laumann, Anthony Palk, Raymond C. Rosen, *Journal of the American Medical Association* 282, 13 (1999), 537–44

'Sexual Behaviour and its Medicalisation: in Sickness and in Health', Graham Hart, Kaye Wellings, *British Medical Journal* 324 (2002), 896–900

Try Weakly
'Problems with Sexual Function in People Attending London General Practitioners: Cross-sectional Study', Irwin Nazareth, Petra Boynton, Michael King, *British Medical Journal* 327 (2003), 425–31

'Sexual Desire Discrepancies: Effects on Sexual and Relationship Satisfaction in Heterosexual Dating Couples', Stephanie Davies, Jennifer Katz, Joan L. Jackson, *Archives of Sexual Behavior*, 28, 6 (1999), 553–68

Dream On
'Power, Desire, and Pleasure in Sexual Fantasies', Eileen L. Zurbriggen, Megan R. Yost, *Journal of Sex Research* 41 (2004), 288–99

'Sexual Fantasies About One's Partner versus Someone Else: Gender Differences in Incidence and Frequency', Thomas V. Hicks, Harold Leitenberg, *Journal of Sex Research* 38 (2001), 43–50

'Gender Differences in the Content of Cognitive Distraction During Sex', Marta Meana, Sarah E. Nunnink, *Journal of Sex Research* 43 (2006), 59–67

Addicted to Love
'Sexual Addiction, Sexual Compulsivity, Sexual Impulsivity, or What?: Toward a Theoretical Model', John Bancroft, Zoran Vukadinovic, *Journal of Sex Research* 41, 3 (2004), 225–34

'How to Recognize the Signs of Sexual Addiction', Jennifer P. Schneider, *Postgraduate Medicine* 90, 6 (1991)

Sex Toys
'Older Women's Sexuality', Lesley A. Yee, Kendra J. Sundquist, *Medical Journal of Australia* 178, 12 (2003), 640–43

'Qualities Midlife Women Desire in Their Sexual Relationships and Their Changing Sexual Response', *Psychology of Women Quarterly* 22, 2 (2006), 285–303

Just for the Celibate
'The Decision to Remain in an Involuntary Celibate Relationship', Denise A. Donnelly, Elisabeth O. Burgess, *Journal of Marriage and Family* 70, 2 (2008), 519–35

It's Width not Length
'Magnetic Resonance Imaging of Male and Female Genitals During Coitus and Female Sexual Arousal', Willibrond Weijmar Schultz, Pek van Andel, Ida Sabelis, Edyard Mooyaart, *British Medical Journal* 319 (1999), 1596–9

'Penile Length in the Flaccid and Erect States: Guidelines for Penile Augmentation', H. Wessells, T. F. Lue, J. W. McAnich, *Journal of Urology* 156, 3 (1996), 995–7

'Penile Length is Normal in Most Men Seeking Penile Lengthening Procedures', N. Mondaini, R. Ponchietti, P. Gontero, G. H. Muir, A. Natali, E. Caldarera, S. Biscioni, M. Rizzo, *International Journal of Impotence Research* 14, 4 (2002), 283–6

Save Sex
Seven Deadly Sins, Economic and Social Research Council, 2005

'Dating Behaviors of University Students', David Knox, Kenneth Wilson, *Family Relations* 30 (1981), 255–8

Neurotic Erotic
'Romantic Partners' Use of Pornography: Its Significance for Women', Ana J. Bridges, Raymond M. Bergner, Matthew Hesson-Mcinnis, *Journal of Sex and Marital Therapy* 29, 1 (2003)

'College Student Attitudes Towards Pornography Use', Sarah O'Reilly, David Knox, Marty E. Zusman, *College Student Journal* 41, 2 (2007), 402–8

Born to Use Porn?
'Sex Differences in Response to Visual Sexual Stimuli: A Review', Heather A. Rupp, Kim Wallen, *Archives of Sexual Behavior* 37, 2 (2008)

'Gender Differences in Pornography Consumption among Young Heterosexual Danish Adults', Gert Martin Held, *Archives of Sexual Behavior* 35, 5 (2006), 577–85

One For the Girls!, Clarissa Smith, Intellect Books, 2007

8. SURVIVING CHILDREN

Bundle of Joy?
'Parenthood and Marital Satisfaction: A Meta-analytic Review', J. M. Twenge, W. K. Campbell, C. A. Foster, *Journal of Marriage and Family* 65, 3 (2003), 574–83

'The Baby and the Marriage: Identifying Factors that Buffer Against Decline in Marital Satisfaction After the First Baby Arrives', Alyson Shapiro, John Gottman, *Journal of Family Psychology* 14, 1, 59–70

'Costs and Rewards of Children: The Effects of Becoming a Parent on Adults' Lives', Khi M. Nomaguchi, Melissa A. Milkie, *Journal of Marriage and Family* 65, 2 (2003), 356–74

'Patterns of Marital Change Across the Transition to Parenthood: Pregnancy to Three Years Postpartum', Jay Belsky, Michael Rovine, *Journal of Marriage and Family* 52, 1 (1990), 5–19

'Marital Perceptions and Interactions Across the Transition to Parenthood', Martha J. Cox, Blair Paley, Margaret Burchinal, C. Chris Payne, *Journal of Marriage and Family* 61, 3 (1999), 611–25

'The Transition to Parenthood: The Magic Moment', One Plus One: www.theparentconnection.org.uk

Changing Minds
'Resident Father's Pregnancy Intentions, Prenatal Behaviors, and Links to Involvement with Infants', Jacinta Bronte-Tinkew, Suzanne Ryan, Jennifer Carrano, Kristin A. Moore, *Journal of Marriage and Family* 69, 4 (2007), 977–90

'Effects of Commitment and Psychological Centrality on Fathering', Kay Pasley, Ted G. Futris, Martie L. Skinner, *Journal of Marriage and Family* 64, 1 (2002), 130–38

'Does Fatherhood Matter for Men?', David J. Eggebeen, Chris Knoester, *Journal of Marriage and Family* 63, 2 (2001), 381–93

Impact of Infertility
'Infertility and Psychological Distress: A Critical Review of the Literature', Arthur L. Griel, paper presented to annual meeting of the Society for the Study of Social Problems, August 1993

'Coping Processes of Couples Experiencing Infertility', Brennan D. Peterson, Christopher R. Newton, Karen H. Rosen, Robert S. Schulman, *Family Relations* 55 (2006), 227–39

'Reconstructing Their Lives: A Longitudinal, Qualitative Analysis of the Transition to Biological Childlessness for Infertile Couples', Judith C. Daniluk, *Journal of Counselling and Development* 79 (2001), 439–49

'Infertility Treatment and Marital Relationships: A 1-year Prospective Study Among Successfully Treated ART Couples and Their Controls', L. Repokari, R.-L. Punamaki, L. Unkila-Kallio, S. Vilska, P. Poikkeus, J.

Sinkkonen, F. Almqvist, A. Tiitinen, M. Tulppala, *Human Reproduction* 22, 5 (2007)

Seasonal Birth Disorders
National Statistics Quarterly, Spring 2001, Stationery Office, 2001

'Seasonal Birth Patterns of Neurological Disorders', E. Fuller Torrey, Judy Miller, Robert Rawlings, Robert H. Yolken, *Neuro-epidemiology* 19, 4 (2000)

'Children Born in the Summer Have Increased Risk for Coeliac Disease', A. Ivarsson, O. Hernell, L. Nystrom, L. A. Pearson, *Journal of Epidemiology and Community Health* 57, 1 (2003), 36–9

'Effects of Month of Birth on the Risk of Suicide', Emad Salib, Mario Cortina-Borja, *British Journal of Psychiatry* 188 (2006), 416–22

'Child Psychiatric Disorder and Relative Age Within School Year: Cross-sectional Survey of Large Population Sample', Robert Goodman, Julia Gledhill, Tasmin Ford, *British Medical Journal* 327 (2003), 472

'Timing of Birth and Risk of Multiple Sclerosis: Population-based Study', Christen J. Willer, David A. Dyment, A. Dessa Sadovnick, Peter M. Rothwell, T. Jock Murray, George C. Eberes, *British Medical Journal* 330 (2005), 120

'Does Month of Birth Affect Risk of Crohn's Disease in Children and Adolescence?', Henrik Toft Sorenson, Lars Pederson, Bente Norgard, Kirsten Fonager, Kenneth J. Rothman, *British Medical Journal* 323 (2001), 907

Kids as Contraceptives
'Sexuality During Pregnancy and the Year Postpartum', Janet Shibley Hyde, John D. DeLamamter, Ashley E. Pant, Janis M. Byrd, *Journal of Sex Research* 33, 2 (1996), 143–52

'Patterns of Marital Change Across the Transition to Parenthood: Pregnancy to Three Years Postpartum', Jay Belsky, Michael Rovine, *Journal of Marriage and Family* 52, 1 (1990), 5–19

Step to Take
'How the Birth of a Child Affects Involvement with Stepchildren', Susan D. Stewart, *Journal of Marriage and Family* 67, 2 (2005), 461–73

'Stepparents' Perception of the Factors Affecting the Quality of the Stepparent/Stepchild Relationship', David A. Adeyemo, Grace Igaba Omongha, *Journal of Human Ecology* 23, 2 (2008), 91–9

Step-parenting in the 1990s, Joseph Rowntree Foundation, Ref 658

'Stepfamilies and Lone Parents: Changing Family Life in Britain', *Economic and Social Research Council*, 2004

For the Kids
The State of our Unions: The Social Health of Marriage in America, 2001, National Marriage Project, Rutgers University

Divorce: Facts, Causes, and Consequences, Ann-Marie Ambert, Vanier Institute of the Family, 2005

'Unhappily Ever After: Effects of Long-term, Low-quality Marriages on Well-being', Daniel N. Hawkins, Alan Booth, *Social Forces* 84, 1 (2005), 451–71

'Delayed Parental Divorce: How Much Do Children Benefit?', *Journal of Marriage and Family* 63, 2 (2001), 446–57

9. TESTING TIMES

First Feelings
You can find Dr Kalish at www.nancykalish.com

'Rekindling Romance: Seniors who Find Lost Loves', Nancy Kalish, Sacramento, www.lostlovers.com/reports.htm

'2001, A Cyberspace Odyssey, Friends and Lovers: Connecting Past and Present Via the Internet', Nancy Kalish, a paper presented to the 109th Annual Convention of the American Psychological Association, 2001

'Adults Who Reunited with Their Adolescent Sweethearts: A Survey', Nancy Kalish, a paper presented to the 108th Annual Convention of the American Psychological Association, 2000

'Fanning Old Flames: Emotional and Cognitive Effects of Suppressing Thoughts of a Past Relationship', M. Wegner-Daniel, B. Gold-Daniel, *Journal of Personality and Social Psychology* 68, 5 (1995), 782–92

Fatal Attraction
'"Be Careful What You Wish for …": A Quantitative and Qualitative Investigation of "Fatal Attraction"', Diane H. Femlee, *Personal Relationships* 5 (1998), 235–53

'The Ups and Downs of Dating: Fluctuations in Satisfaction in Newly Formed Romantic Relationships', Ximena B. Arriaga, *Journal of Personality and Social Psychology* 80, 5 (2001), 754–65

Fingers to the Bone
'The Division of Labour and Perceptions of Parental Roles: Lesbian Couples Across the Transition to Parenthood', Abbie E. Goldberg,

Maureen Perry-Jenkins, *Journal of Social and Personal Relationships* 24, 2 (2007); 297–319

'Benefits of Equitable Relationships: The Impact of Sense of Fairness, Household Division of Labor, and Decision Making Power on Perceived Social Support', Merieke Van Willigen, Patricia Drentea, *Sex Roles*, 2001

'The Allocation Within the Family: Welfare Implications of Life in a Couple', Helen Couprie, *Economic Journal* 117, 516 (2007), 287–305

'Men's Changing Contribution to Housework and Childcare', Oriel Sullivan, Scott Coltrane, a paper presented to the 11th Annual Conference of the Council on Contemporary Families, 2008

'Research on Household Labor: Modeling and Measuring the Social Embeddedness of Routine Family Work', Scott Coltrane, *Journal of Marriage and Family* 62, 4 (2004), 1208–33

'Modern Marriage', Pew Research: http://pewresearch.org/pubs/542/modern-marriage

Nag or Negotiate?
'Demand-Withdraw Communication in Marital Interaction: Tests of Interspousal Contingency and Gender Role Hypotheses', Nadya A. Klinetob, David A. Smith, *Journal of Marriage and Family* 58, 4 (1996), 945–57

'Nonconscious Relationship Reactance', Tanya L. Chartrand, Amy N. Dalton, Gavan Fitzsimons, *Journal of Experimental Social Psychology* 43 (2007)

Who Moans Most?
'Gender Differences in Standards for Romantic Relationships', Anita L. Vangelisti, John A. Daly, *Personal Relationships* 4, 3 (1997), 203–19

'Wives' Domain-specific "Marriage Work" with Friends and Spouses: Links to Marital Quality', Christine M. Proulx, Heather M. Helms, C. Chris Payne, *Family Relations* 53, 4 (2004), 393–404

Too Many Toddies?
'Alcohol Problems in Intimate Relationships: Identification and Intervention', National Institute on Alcohol Abuse and Alcoholism: http://pubs.niaaa.nih.gov/publications/niaaa-guide/index.htm

'Alcohol Use Disorders in Elderly People: Fact or Fiction?', Karim Dar, *British Journal of Psychiatry* 12 (2006), 173–181

'Alcohol Misuse Among Older People', Alcohol Concern: www.alcoholconcern.org.uk/servlets/doc/50

'We' Time
'Implications of Overwork and Overload for the Quality of Men's Family Relationships', Ann C. Crouter, Matthew F. Bumpus, Melissa R. Head, Susan M. McHale, *Journal of Marriage and Family* 63, 2 (2001), 404–16

Married Only at the Weekends? A Study of the Amount of Time Spent Together by Spouses, Reg Gatenby, Office for National Statistics, 2001

'Britain's Views on Family and Community', ICM poll for Equal Opportunity Commission, 2007

'Leisure-activity Patterns and Marital Satisfaction: A Further Test', Thomas B. Holman, Mary Jacquart, *Journal of Marriage and Family* 50, 1 (1988), 69–77

'Sexually Inactive Marriages', D. Donnelly, *Journal of Sex Research* 30, 2 (1993), 171–8

Income-linked Divorce
'When She Earns More Than He Does: A Longitudinal Study of Dual-earner Couples', Robert T. Brennan, Rosalind-Chait Barnett, Karen C. Gareis, *Journal of Marriage and Family* 63, 1 F (2001), 168–82

'Changes in Wives' Income: Effects on Marital Happiness, Psychological Well-being, and the Risk of Divorce', Stacy J. Rogers, Danelle D. DeBoer, *Journal of Marriage and Family* 63, 2 (2001), 458–72

'The Impact of Husbands' and Wives' Relative Earnings on Marital Disruption', D. Alex Heckert, Thomas C. Nowak, K. A. Snyder, *Journal of Marriage and Family* 60, 3 (1998), 690–703

'Effects of Changing Material Circumstances on the Incidence of Marital Breakdown', Fiona McAllister, in *High Divorce Rates: The State of the Evidence on Reasons and Remedies*, Family Policy Studies Unit, 1999

Outlaw the In-laws?
'Daughters-in-law and Mothers-in-law Seeking Their Place Within the Family: A Qualitative Study of Differing Viewpoints', M. Jean Turner, Carolyn R. Young, Kelly I. Black, *Family Relations* 55 (2006), 588–600

'The Influence of In-laws on Change in Marital Success', Chalandra M. Bryant, Rand D. Conger, Jennifer M. Meehan, *Journal of Marriage and Family* 63, 3 (2001), 614–26

Pathetic Presents
'The Mismeasure of Love: How Self-doubt Contaminates Relationship Beliefs', Sandra L. Murray, John G. Holmes, Dale W. Griffin, Gina Bellavia, Paul Rose, *Personality and Social Psychology Bulletin* 27, 4 (2001), 423–36

'The Social Dimensions of Gift Behaviour', David J. Cheal, *Journal of Social and Personal Relationships* 3, 4 (1986), 423–39

Question of Misery
'Coping Difficulty in Men Following Their Partner's Miscarriage: An Evolutionary Explanation', Lisa Rauschmeier: www.oswego. edu/~rauschme/evolutionary3.doc

'Miscarriage Effects on Couples' Interpersonal and Sexual Relationships During the First Year After Loss: Women's Perceptions', Kristen M. Swanson, Zahra A. Karmali, Suzanne H. Powell, Faina Pulvermakher, *Psychosomatic Medicine* 65 (2003), 902–10

'Grief and Depression After Miscarriage: Their Separation, Antecedents, and Course', Manfred Beutel, Rainer Deckardt, Michael von Rad, Herbert Weiner, *Psychosomatic Medicine* 57 (1995), 517–26

'Men and Miscarriage', Miscarriage Association: http://www. miscarriageassociation.org.uk/ma2006/information/leaflets/menmisc.pdf

'Pregnancy Loss: A Major Life Event Affecting Emotional Health and Well Being', Philip M. Boyce, John T. Condon, David A. Ellwood, *Medical Journal of Australia*, 178 (2002), 250–51

'Major Depressive Disorder in the 6 Months After Miscarriage', R. Neugebauer, J. Kline, A. Skodol, P. O'Connor, P. A. Geller, Z. Stein, M. Susser, *Journal of the American Medical Association* 277, 5 (1997), 383–8

Having Your Cake
'Spousal Alternatives and Marital Dissolution', Scott South, Kim Lloyd, *American Sociological Review* 60, 1 (1995), 21–36

10. HAPPILY EVER AFTER

Not Just a Film
'The Proportion of Marriages Ending in Divorce', B. Wilson, S. Smallwood, *Popular Trends* 131 (2008)

'The Nature and Predictors of the Trajectory of Change in Marital Quality for Husbands and Wives Over the First 10 Years of Marriage', Lawrence A. Kurdek, *Developmental Psychology* 35, 5 (1999), 1283–96

Cohabitation, Marriage, and Trajectories in Well-being and Relationships, Kelly Musick, Larry Bumpass, California Center for Population Research, 2006

Re-examining the Case of Marriage: Variation and Change in Well-being and Relationships, Kelly Musick, Larry Bumpass, California Center for Population Research, September 2007

'Decade Review: Observing Marital Interaction', John Gottman, Clifford I. Notarius, *Journal of Marriage and Family* 62, 4 (2000), 862–79

'Understanding and Altering the Longitudinal Course of Marriage', Thomas N. Bradbury, Benjamin R. Karney, *Journal of Marriage and Family* 66 (2004), 862–79

Leaving the Nest
'Mothers' and Fathers' Perceptions of Change and Continuity in Their Relationships with Young Adult Sons and Daughters', Christine M. Proulx, Heather M. Helms, *Journal of Family Issues* 29, 2 (2008), 234–261

'Empty Nest or Revolving Door? A Prospective Study of Women's Quality of Life in Midlife During the Phase of Children Leaving and Re-entering the Home', L. Dennerstein, E. Dudley, J. Guthrie, *Psychological Medicine* 32 (2002), 545–50

'Effects of Empty Nest Transition on Self-Report of Psychological and Physical Well-Being', Elizabeth Bates Harkins, *Journal of Marriage and Family* 40, 3 (1978), 549–56

'Economic Independence, Economic Status, and Empty Nest in Midlife Marital Disruption', Bridget Hiedemann, Olga Suhomlinova, Angela M. O'Rand, *Journal of Marriage and Family* 60, 1 (1998), 219–31

Redundancy Recovery
'Lost Jobs, Broken Marriages', Marcus Eliason, Working Papers of the Institute for Social and Economic Research, paper 2004–21

'Socio-demographic Predictors of Divorce', Lynda Clarke, Ann Berrington, in *High Divorce Rates: The State of the Evidence on Reasons and Remedies*, Volume 1, Lord Chancellor's Department

Sofa So Good?
Unhappy Marriages: Does Counselling Help?, Kieran McKeown, Pauline Lehane, Trutz Haase, Jonathan Pratschke, Report to ACCORD, Kieran McKeown Limited, 2002

'How Useful is Relationship Therapy?', John Simons, in *High Divorce Rates: The State of the Evidence On Reasons and Remedies*, Volume 2, Lord Chancellor's Department; London

'Towards Understanding the Reasons for Divorce', Ilene Wolcott, Jody Hughes, Working Paper No 20, Australian Institute of Family Studies, 1999

Remarriage Rush
'The Desire to Date and Remarry Among Older Widows and Widowers', Deborah Carr, *Journal of Marriage and Family* 66, 4 (2004), 1051–68

'Gender Differences in New Partnership Choices and Constraints for Older Widows and Widowers', Kate Davidson, *Aging International* 27, 4 (2002), 43–60

'Dating and Remarriage Over the First Two Years of Widowhood', Schneider Danielle, *Annals of Clinical Psychiatry* 8, 2 (1996), 51–7

'Repartnering After First Union Disruption', Zheng Wu, Christopher M. Schimmele, *Journal of Marriage and Family* 67, 1 (2005), 27–36

Menopausal Madness
'Changing Menopausal Bodies: How Women Think and Act in the Face of a Reproductive Transition and Gendered Beauty Ideals', Heather Dillaway, *Sex Roles* 53 (2005)

'Myths and Realities of the Menopause', Karen A. Matthews, *Psychosomatic Medicine* 54 (1992)

The Female Brain, Louhann Brizendine, Bantam Press, 2007

Keeping Mum
'Marriage as Support or Strain? Marital Quality Following the Death of a Parent', Debra Umberson, *Journal of Marriage and Family* 57 (1995), 709–23

'Marital Dissatisfaction, Psychological Distress, and the Coping of Parents of Pediatric Cancer Patients', J. E. H. M. Hoekstra-Webers, J. P. C. Jaspers, W. A. Kamps, E. C. Klip, *Journal of Marriage and Family* 60, 4 (1998), 1012–21

Many Happy Retirements
Aspects of Retirement for Older Women, Australian Government Office for Women, 2006

'Retirement and Marital Decision Making: Effects on Retirement Satisfaction', Maximilliane E. Szinovacz, Adam Davey *Journal of Marriage and Family* 67, 2 (2005), 387–98

'"I Married Him for Better or Worse but not for Lunch": Retirement and Marriage', David de Vaus, Yvonne Wells. Paper presented to the 8th Australian Family Research Conference, Melbourne, Australia, 2003

Renegotiating Identity and Relationships: Men and Women's Adjustments to Retirement, Helen Barnes, Jane Parry, PSI Discussion Paper 14, Policy Studies Institute, 2003

Ache of Hearts
'Neurohumoral Features of Myocardial Stunning Due to Sudden Emotional Stress', Han S. Wittstein, David R. Thiermann, Joao A. C.

Lima, Kenneth L. Baughman, Steven P. Shulman *et al*, *New England Journal of Medicine* 352, 6 (2005), 539–48

'Broken Heart: A Statistical Study of Increased Mortality Among Widowers', C. Murray Parkes, R. Benjamin, R. G. Fitzgerald, *British Medical Journal* 1 (1969), 740–43

'The Broken Heart Syndrome', Ilan S. Wittstein, *Cleveland Clinic Journal of Medicine* 74, suppl 1 (2007)

Everlasting Love
'Secular Trends in Self-reported Sexual Activity and Satisfaction in Swedish 70-year olds: Cross-sectional Survey of Four Populations, 1971–2001', Nils Beckman, Magda Waern, Deborah Gustafson, Ingmar Skoog, *British Medical Journal*, 337 (2008)

Married People: Staying Together in the Age of Divorce, F. Klagsbrun, Bantam Books, 1985

Til' Death Do Us Part, J. C. Lauer, R. H. Lauer, Haworth Press, 1986

10 Lessons to Transform Your Marriage, John M. Gottman, Julie Schwartz Gottman, Joan DeClaire, Three Rivers Press, 2006

Why Marriages Last: a Discussion of the Literature, Robyn Parker, Australian Institute of Family Studies, 2002

'Long-term Marriage: Age, Gender and Satisfaction', Robert W. Levenson, Laura L. Carstensen, John M. Gottman, *Psychology and Aging*, 8, 2 (1993)

Index